"Sara Barratt wants to start a riot. An uproar. A disturbance for Jesus. Unlike some teenagers who want to disrupt and destroy, she wants to bravely build. With *Love Riot*, she is calling apathetic bystanders around the church to become wholehearted followers of Christ. She is actively driving and motivating her generation to live with reckless abandon because of God's great love. Undoubtedly, when you read, you will be captivated by her unrestrained outburst of irresistible faith."

Kyle Idleman, author of *Not a Fan* and *Don't Give Up* and senior pastor of Southeast Christian Church

"God is at work among my generation. There's no denying that, especially after reading *Love Riot*. In this passionate plea to fellow teenagers, Sara calls us to join her in rebelling against spiritual apathy and choosing instead to wholeheartedly follow Jesus, no matter the cost. This book will challenge you, encourage you, and ignite your pursuit of Christ. I highly recommend it!"

Jaquelle Crowe Ferris, author of *This Changes Everything*

"Every teenager needs to read this book. *Love Riot* will challenge your idea of what it means to be a teen that truly follows Christ. Sara Barratt raises the bar and calls her peers to a higher standard. This book has the power to change lives!"

Kristen Clark and Bethany Beal, authors of *Sex, Purity, and the Longings of a Girl's Heart* and cofounders of GirlDefined Ministries

"*Love Riot* calls the teenagers of the world to step up and step out in their faith and cause a riot against the low expectations set for youth across the globe. It may be aimed at one generation, but *Love Riot* has the ability to cause the riot it's intending through the hearts of the young to the old."

Riley Banks-Snyder, auth

"If you're searching for a book that teaches you how to play it safe as a Christian teen, this probably isn't the book for you. If you're searching for a book that teaches you how to live for both God and the world, this isn't for you. But if you're a teen who longs to make your parents' faith personal—or if you're searching to understand the value of church and God in the first place—then this is the book you've been searching for. I couldn't be more thrilled to see a teen challenging the status quo and setting an example for her peers to follow. It's my prayer that this book will prompt teens to live boldly and passionately and to rebel against the low expectations of their generation. If readers will follow Sara's lead, there will be no stopping this generation from making a positive impact on their society. This could perhaps spark the beginning of a revolution. A cultural awakening. A love riot by teens who are simply in pursuit of their loving Savior, Jesus Christ."

Tessa Emily Hall, author of *Coffee Shop Devos* and *Love Your Selfie*

"Sara Barratt's *Love Riot* reminds me of a saying my pastor taught me. 'If your version of Christianity doesn't cost you anything, you've got the bootleg.' In this book, Sara boldly calls Christ followers to drop the bootleg version of Christianity and pick up their cross. With radical love and reckless abandon, we can begin to run toward the revival of our hearts in Jesus."

Megan Brown, author of *Esther: Come Out of Hiding*

love riot

love riot

A Teenage Call to Live with Relentless Abandon for Christ

Sara Barratt

BakerBooks

a division of Baker Publishing Group
Grand Rapids, Michigan

© 2020 by Sara Barratt

Published by Baker Books
a division of Baker Publishing Group
PO Box 6287, Grand Rapids, MI 49516-6287
www.bakerbooks.com

Printed in the United States of America

Library of Congress Cataloging-in-Publication Data
Names: Barratt, Sara, 1999– author.
Title: Love riot : a teenage call to live with relentless abandon for Christ / Sara
    Barratt.
Description: Grand Rapids, Michigan : Baker Books, a division of Baker Publishing
    Group, 2020. | Includes bibliographical references.
Identifiers: LCCN 2019034518 | ISBN 9780801094408 (paperback)
Subjects: LCSH: Christian teenagers—Religious life.
Classification: LCC BV4531.3 .B365 2020 | DDC 248.8/3—dc23
LC record available at https://lccn.loc.gov/2019034518

ISBN: 978-1-5409-0089-0 (casebound)

In keeping with biblical principles of
creation stewardship, Baker Publishing Group advocates the responsible
use of our natural resources. As a
member of the Green Press Initia-
tive, our company uses recycled
paper when possible. The text paper
of this book is composed in part of
post-consumer waste.

20   21   22   23   24   25   26   7   6   5   4   3   2   1

For all who have gone out, boldly
proclaiming the name of Jesus.
For all who have believed that to live
is Christ, and to die is gain.
For all who have loved much . . . and sacrificed much.
For all who have lifted the cross and not looked back.
May we not forget their passion or give up in
freedom what was bought through persecution.

And for my mom . . . the person who's taught me more about following Jesus than anyone else. You inspire me. I love you!

Soli Deo Gloria

contents

foreword

My life changed when I was sixteen. I remember sitting down at my desk, agitated and desperate. My future hung in the balance. I could feel it. God was tugging on my heart, and my sinful desires were tugging back. I needed to make a choice.

Hunched over my laptop, I began to type.

> Will I choose the fate of the common man or that of the uncommon man?
>
> Needless to say, a life of sin and sorrow is readily available to all, whereas a life of purity, honor, and virtue is only granted to a precious few. . . .
>
> The path of the righteous man is overgrown and seldom used. It is a lonely road, often uphill and through deep valleys. The common way offers many amenities, it is a well-worn path, easily traveled and with plenty of company.
>
> Righteousness is work comprised of fleeing from temptation, running to Christ, fighting the good fight, running the race, and wrestling with myself.
>
> Complacency, however, offers a road devoid of care. I give myself to the very things I should flee from and fight with. So much easier to choose, so much simpler, and just what we want—yet not what I want.[1]

As the words spilled out, my resolve grew stronger. I wanted to please God. I wanted to live for Him. I didn't want to be another complacent teenager. I didn't want sin to reign in my life. Even though my sinful desires were still present, I couldn't follow both them and God.

Fourteen years later, I can report with tears that God honored this passionate outpouring of my young heart. He kept his side of the bargain, responding to my youthful zeal with steadfast love and faithfulness, drawing me back again and again. Typing those words didn't end the battle, but it did settle the outcome. Looking back I would call that day—August 8, 2005—the most important day of my life. It was the day I began to seek the Lord in earnest.

The Bible is filled with these stories of transformation. Did you know David was writing psalms and slaying giants as a teenager?[2] Or that Jeremiah was seventeen when he accepted God's call to be a prophet?[3] Or that many of the disciples were teenagers when they left their fishing nets to follow Jesus?[4]

I recently learned that Josiah, who became king at eight years old, began to seek the Lord at sixteen. The Bible shares this short account of Josiah's early life, "In the eighth year of his reign, while he was still young, he began to seek the God of his father David" (2 Chron. 34:3). Before he began repairing the temple, before he rediscovered the Book of the Law, before he destroyed idol worship in Israel—Josiah began to seek the Lord. I've heard this story many times but never caught this detail. It is the first significant event of Josiah's reign, and it set the stage for everything else.

While he was still young, he began to seek the Lord.

What about you? Have you started to seek? Are you seeking earnestly? Nothing matters more than this. God is not looking for a perfect GPA, a state championship, or a college scholarship. "The Lord looks down from heaven on all mankind to see if there are any who understand, any who seek God" (Ps. 14:2 NIV).

Will you be one of them? Will I?

Reading *Love Riot* has challenged me, because I've grown satisfied in my relationship with God. Like Sara describes, I think I'm seeking hard, but in reality, I'm hardly seeking. In the past, I read the whole Bible in two months, memorized the entire book of 1 John, and set an alarm and prayed every ten minutes for a week. These weren't religious tricks to impress anyone; they were genuine expressions of my heart to know and love God—and I want to be intentional like that again.

This book is an invitation to seek the Lord with all our hearts. No more, "Wait till you're older." No more, "Wait till life calms down." No more waiting. Period.

For myself, I choose to stop waiting to pursue more of God's presence through prayer. For years I've used the excuse that my circumstances are too difficult, stressful, and unpredictable to spend a lot of time in prayer. After all, we tend to think we need a consistent schedule to develop a good prayer routine. But the Bible sets us straight: "Is anyone among you suffering? Let him pray" (James 5:13). And so I will.

Today I recommit to seeking *hard*. Will you join me?

Brett Harris, coauthor of *Do Hard Things*

introduction

it's time for a love riot

There's a new generation arising.

Some call us iGen or Generation Z. Others refer to us as post-millennials. We're the heartbeat of this century. We're known as coffee shop loving, selfie taking, video game playing, fun-loving individuals. We're tech-savvy and hip and have a reputation for knowing what's trendy and cool.

Who are we? We're teenagers.

If you haven't noticed, a lot of people have a lot of opinions about us. But few automatically label us as passionate Jesus followers.

I'm out to change that.

I'm nineteen years old. That means I've officially been a teenager for seven years. In other words, you could say I know a bit about this thing called "teenagehood."

I know the stigma attached to our age bracket. I'm familiar with the low expectations and the fact that culture expects us to be selfish, irresponsible, and rebellious. I've walked beside teenagers battling these expectations, and I also know what it's like to have people expect *me* to give in to the pressure. But there's one thing that sets me apart—*Jesus*. He has profoundly, radically, 100 percent changed my life.

I'm really not much different than any other teenager. I still struggle. Every day I battle things like impure thoughts and arrogance. I wrestle with pride and unforgiveness. By all accounts, because of my humanity, I should be (and often am) selfish and self-focused, *but Jesus* is teaching me how to be selfless. I should be utterly irresponsible, *but Jesus* is equipping me and giving me responsibilities as a member of His kingdom. I should be totally rebellious, *but Jesus* is leading me to live out a different kind of rebellion—a rebellion against the sin and brokenness in our world. *But* and *Jesus* are two of the most powerful words put together. They're the ultimate game changer. They flip dissatisfaction to satisfaction, nonfulfillment to fulfillment, a life of pointless striving and searching to a passionate pursuit of Jesus Christ. I know because I've experienced this glorious redemption. I don't deserve any of it. I'm just a normal teenage girl chasing God with everything in me.

Am I all the way there? No.

Am I perfect? Absolutely not.

God doesn't need perfect people, but He does want passionate people.

And that's what I think is missing from our generation.

The *passion*. The *challenge*. The radical, crazy kind of love that can flip your life upside down.

Throughout my years in church and hanging out at youth group, I've noticed this void in myself and in the teens around me. I knew there had to be more—more passion, devotion, and commitment—when it came to following Jesus.

So I began searching and questioning myself and other teens but mostly the status quo we lived by. I started writing, pouring my heart and questions into blog posts and articles, and I found that I am not the only one. I discovered that there is more—much more—to following Jesus. Not only do teens sense this void but they also know Jesus is calling them to a more radical faith—they just need the challenge and courage to step up and live it out.

I kept searching, seeking Jesus, and writing. One by one God opened doors. From leading a small group for preteen girls to becoming lead writer and editor for TheRebelution.com—one of the most popular websites for Christian teens—I found myself jumping outside my comfort zone and learning to live out the things I was writing. I'm still searching and seeking Jesus (and I'm obviously still writing). Because the more I interact with other teens, both online and face-to-face, the more excited I become about our generation learning to wholeheartedly follow Christ. But in order for that to happen, we need to be strengthened, inspired, and even *dared* in our walk with God.

Throughout this book, you'll get to know teens who have wrestled with the same questions and doubts you have.

Girls like Bella, who was raised in a Christian family but is still looking for answers. Outwardly doing everything right but inwardly desperate and seeking.

Or Meghan, who once followed Jesus but is now caught in a downward spiral, trying everything to regain joy and peace.

You'll also meet some of my personal heroes.

Ivan, who was unwilling to deny Christ but willing to die for Him instead.

Jim, who was passionate about spreading the gospel—no matter the cost.

Jeremiah, a warrior who battled for the lives of the unborn—even as he fought for his own.

You'll learn about my journey. Why Jesus means so much to me and why I'm following Him, even though it's not always easy. You'll hear about the things I struggle with and the times I've failed, but more importantly, all the times Jesus has been faithful.

And together we'll dig into why these things matter.

Whether you have no idea why you're even reading this book, whether you're burned out on yet another stereotypical youth group pizza party and game night and crave something deeper, whether you're tired of trying so hard and never feeling good enough, or whether you simply want to get to know Jesus better, we'll dig beneath the surface and learn why following Him is so important.

If you're tired of empty seeking . . .

Don't understand what being a Christian is all about . . .

Want to leave low expectations and apathy in the dust . . .

Are hungry for more of Jesus . . .

Then it's time for a love riot.

What Is a Love Riot?

It's time to start a riot against our own apathy.

Our relationship with God is so safe. Do you sense it? There's no daring. It doesn't cost us anything. Most Christians are content with blending in—but it's time to step out. We're on the brink of a revolution, a holy uprising, a *love riot* that can launch us from apathetic bystanders to wholehearted followers.

As I look back on my own relationship with Jesus, I notice two pivotal things.

Passion and *commitment*.

A thriving relationship with Christ needs both. If you have only passion, it will flicker out when the going gets tough, when criticism and persecution come, and when hard decisions need to be made. It might be enough at first, but all on its own, passion isn't sustainable.

And if you have only commitment, your relationship with Christ will be less a relationship and more a religion—a commitment to the dos and don'ts of being a Christian. It lacks what Jesus tells us is the first and greatest commandment—love for God.

Passion and commitment go hand in hand. They're bound together for the faithful Jesus follower. Passion leads to commitment, and commitment sustains passion. I echo the words of Elisabeth Elliot, "I have one desire now—to live a life of reckless abandon for the Lord, putting all my energy and strength into it."[1]

That's what following Jesus is all about. Awakening a passion— a relentless abandon—for Christ, and backing it up with something that will last.

In a word, it's *devotion.*

Real, radical devotion is about more than temporary enthusiasm.

God doesn't want our flash-in-the-pan enthusiasm. Our "here one day, gone the next" kind of love. That's not what Christianity is about. That's not what this book is about.

It's about die-hard commitment.

It's about tenacious faith.

It's about radical obedience.

It's about falling *in love* with Jesus.

Today, I invite you to join me on a journey away from the world and toward Christ.

I can't promise it'll be easy. In fact, it might be incredibly painful. It'll stretch you and challenge you, but I can guarantee it'll change you. It's not for the faint of heart. Instead, it's for the revolutionaries and the prodigals and the rebel inside of you saying, "There's gotta be more." You might be called crazy or weird, maybe even a Jesus freak. You might be excluded, ridiculed, or persecuted. The stakes are great, but the reward is far greater.

It's time to discover it. To lay down your pursuit of everything else, and instead run after the One who has everything you need. It's time for a reawakening and a revival.

What kind of passion do you need to transform your life?

How radical are you willing to get?

What kind of love will it take to make you give your all?

Let's start this love riot.

PART ONE

the call

1

revealing the counterfeit

what's the problem?

You each get fifty dollars to spend however you like," my youth leader announced as we stood along the church hallway, waiting for a few stragglers to arrive. He passed out small Ziploc bags with a few bills inside. It was our church's annual "free money" event, and the youth group had been looking forward to it for weeks. After all, we weren't just handed fifty dollars every day.

"What if we don't spend it all?" one of the teen guys standing across from me asked jokingly. The guy next to him laughed and opened his money bag.

"You'll have to turn in your receipts at the end of the day. If you don't spend the whole fifty, you have to give back what's left."

The guys turned to each other and started discussing plans for the day. They were going to save most of their money until they reached the video game store. We girls, however, were more interested in heading to the mall.

The nearest large town was an hour away. From my seat in the back of the van, I had plenty of opportunity to observe the other teenagers. Everyone was laughing, joking, passing snacks back and forth, and sharing how they were going to spend their money. Halfway there, my heart broke a little as I began to realize what we were actually spending the day doing.

I sat in the back seat, staring out the fogged-over window, as conviction pricked my heart. The entire day—from the money we were given to the places we were headed to the movie we'd watch later—revolved around *us*. None of us thought twice about using the church's money to fund a day indulging ourselves. But was this really the best we could do with our time and money? Was this what being a Christian teen was all about? Was this what being a part of the church was all about? And the worst part: we didn't think anything of it, because this was only one event of many just like it. Events like these were the fabric of our youth group and what we came to church for—to have fun, practice our ping-pong skills, and eat pizza. This was the Christianity we had embraced.

As I continued to ponder these things, I pulled out the tiny notebook I keep in my purse and wrote down five questions.

- What if, instead of a van full of fun, we were a van full of purpose?
- What if, instead of channeling our energy into selfish things, we used it for selfless things?
- What if we chose God's desires over our desires?
- What if we ditched the status quo and arose as a generation proclaiming Jesus?
- What if, one by one, we chose to give up a youth occupied with fulfilling ourselves in exchange for fulfilling the kingdom of God?

What if?

What if we did that today? What if you and I rose above the low expectations of our culture and passionately pursued Christ?

That day, while we shopped, those questions kept ringing in my heart. I came home with a stack of books, but more importantly, I came home with a mountain of conviction. I never went on another "free money" shopping trip again.

Revealing Apathy

Meet Brayden. He's eighteen and a college freshman. Even though he grew up in church, he recently told me, "I've never pursued a passionate relationship with Christ, because I've never had anyone to share it with. No one else I know takes God seriously."

Sixteen-year-old Trevor feels the same way. Struggling with his own distant relationship with God, he reached out to me. "I feel like something's missing. I know God is real. I've seen Him work in other people's lives, but I can't seem to find the strength to change, so I've just kind of put God on the back burner."

Kelly is fifteen years old. She's been in church all her life but notices the issues within its walls. "Christians can be so arrogant when it comes to tough questions," she commented. "Don't give us trite replies or a watered-down message. We need solid answers."

These are real teens just like you and me. These are real problems we face.

Teenagers are struggling. We have questions and doubts about God and Christianity. We see problems in the church and hypocrisy in Christians. We're hungry for truth but rarely given it. Many of us are disgusted with the lukewarm religion we see around us and find it hard to fight against the daily pressure to compromise.

When it comes to Christianity, a lot of teens find themselves at an impasse. Many have walked away from God. Most don't claim a relationship with Him at all. Even those who profess to be

Christians often aren't serious in their commitment. According to the Barna Group, three out of five teens will disconnect from church after the age of fifteen.[1]

If you're a Christian, I'm sure you can relate to the struggles teens like Brayden, Trevor, and Kelly are facing. We all notice that things often aren't the way they should be—in ourselves and in the world around us. There's inconsistency in what we proclaim versus how we live. Like Trevor, we don't feel like we have the strength to change, so we push it all to the back of our minds.

I've been that teenager. The one who was only in church because my parents brought me. The one who didn't have a personal, intimate relationship with God. That "free money" shopping trip was one of the first times my eyes were opened to the fact that there is a problem—not just in the church, or even the event itself, but in *me*. In the way I related to God and church and how I approached my relationship with both. I wasn't serious or committed. I knew something was wrong, and I wanted a more passionate and genuine relationship with Jesus. But none of my peers seemed to have a strong connection with God either, so I didn't know what to do. Can you relate?

There are thousands of teenagers who have given in to low expectations and fallen into the trap of believing our teen years don't matter and that a relationship with God doesn't matter. We might go to church, believe in God, do all the right things (most of the time), but we don't pursue Christ. We're just ordinary teenagers, hanging out in church buildings and at youth groups. We're not putting in our all. Oh, we might think we are. We might think we're doing enough, but deep in our souls we know we have so much more we could give.

I know it.

You know it.

We're passionate teens with a passionless faith, who claim to serve a passionate God in a passionless church.

Something needs to change.

Excuseless Christianity

The church isn't feeding me.

My parents don't teach me about God.

Christians are hypocrites.

The pressure from my friends is too strong.

I don't have time.

I'll get serious about God later.

It really isn't my fault if I'm not actively pursuing Christ. No one else seems to care, so why should I?

Sadly, for many teens, these excuses hold truth. We aren't receiving the spiritual nourishment and challenge we need. Many people who call themselves Christians *do* live hypocritical lives. The pressure to conform to what we see in the world *is* strong. This makes it even harder and more countercultural to passionately follow Christ.

So many teens are leaving the church and walking away from Christianity because we don't make an intimate, personal relationship with Jesus a priority, and we often don't see it modeled for us. We settle for a counterfeit, watered-down gospel that's packaged nicely enough to get our attention. We're content with Jesus on a smartphone, Jesus on a big screen, Jesus inside a fun program, but we don't pursue the pure, undiluted truths of the gospel that are simply . . . Jesus. As a result, church, prayer, and Bible study become part of our "Christian culture" instead of the result of a genuine relationship with Christ. Yes, we might be in church, but are our hearts in Christ?

We have an extremely important task in front of us. Not only are we currently a part of the church, we *are* the future church. Right now, we're dying. Spiritually speaking, our generation is not thriving and growing. Teens like Brayden, Trevor, Kelly, you, and I are the leaders of the future church and an important part of the current church. Does our present walk with God reflect authentic Christianity? Isn't it time for a change? Doesn't it start with us and a teenage reawakening of passion for Christ? What we need, and what the current and future church needs, is a generation of teenagers who are passionately in love with Jesus Christ.

In his well-known book *Crazy Love*, author Francis Chan says, "The world needs Christians who don't tolerate the complacency of their own lives."[2] We've tolerated our own complacency long enough. We've made excuses long enough. The time for change is now. The moment to rise up and reject apathy and pursue Christ has come.

The low expectations may not change. Our external circumstances may not change. But we can.

Our friends may not understand and our peers may not agree, but we can take a stand, rip off the cloak of complacency, and learn to live wholeheartedly for Jesus in spite of it all. Yes, it will be hard. But I believe it's worth it.

I have a vision for my generation. I can see us rising up to be the most devoted, most committed, most passionate generation of Jesus followers the world has ever seen. Beneath the surface lies a dormant passion for God. We just need to wake it up.

I believe it's possible, because thousands of teenagers throughout the centuries have stood up and broken the mold. They've altered the pattern and refused to give in to the pressure. You'll meet some of them in this book. We can follow in their footsteps as we learn to follow Christ *as teenagers*.

It's Time to Make a Choice

I've struggled in my faith. I've wondered if it was worth it. I've had doubts. I've seen hypocrisy and sin in my heart, and it's been ugly. I've thought, *I'm too messed up. I'll never be good enough. Why even try? It would be easier to go with the world.*

But no matter how much I doubt or how often I struggle, I always come back to one thing.

Jesus is worth it. I choose Christ.

I've felt His love and it's overridden my doubt. I've known His forgiveness and it's overthrown my sin. I've experienced His healing and it's eclipsed my pain. I'm not perfect. But I'm now at a place where, even if everyone I know—all my family and friends—turned away from Jesus, I would still follow Him. He's worth that much to me and means more than anything else. This book isn't an indifferent, theological argument but a soul-deep cry from my heart to yours.

I want to share what I'm learning and how I'm falling in love with Jesus, but in order for you to understand and join me on this journey, you have to realize there's a problem and recognize how it has shown up in your life. Let me ask you a few questions. Have you ever

tried to get as close to sin as you could without feeling guilty?

been bored by church and thought it didn't matter?

compromised your standards to fit in with your peers?

put your relationship with God on the back burner?

rebelled against your parents, even when you know they had your best interests in mind?

been more interested in having fun than serving God?

Sound familiar? I've done each and every one of those things. Indifference in our relationship with God shows up in small areas: turning to our phones instead of our Bibles, caring more about the cute girl or guy sitting in front of us in church than what the pastor is preaching, venting to our friends instead of bringing our problems to God. Been there, done that.

Every day you make a choice. Will you live for God, yourself, or try to walk a tightrope between the two? Eventually there comes a point where you have to choose once and for all. It comes down to three options:

You can be an "actor Christian" and settle for a counterfeit faith. Like the actors in your favorite movies, you say the correct things, dress the part, and live by the script. But in reality, you're just a performer playing a role. You might think this option gives you the best of both worlds, but it's a temporary choice. This path is a detour; it eventually leads you to a crossroad between the next two options.

You can give up on Christianity and walk away from God. You can do what you want without feeling guilty and not worry about pursuing a relationship with God. This is the most traveled path, so it's wide and smooth and easy to find—but it's also paved with regret and dissatisfaction. C. S. Lewis, a former atheist turned theologian, wrote, "God can't give us peace and happiness apart from Himself, because there is no such thing."[3] Maybe you've searched for peace and happiness without God. Was it everything you thought it would be?

You can choose Jesus. You can decide to follow Him no matter what and live sold out for His glory. You can invite Jesus into your heart and life, acknowledging your sin and accepting His forgiveness and salvation. Even if you've already accepted Christ as your Savior, you can rededicate your life and commit to following Him. This path is much narrower and harder to find. It's not smooth, but you'll have a personal Guide with you every step of the way. It's a hard path, but it's one filled with joy, peace, and love. It's worth every step of the journey.

Right now I want you to stop and read over those choices again. Which path have you chosen in the past? Which path will you choose today? Think hard and choose carefully, because this choice goes deeper than a quick circle around a, b, or c. This choice is life changing.

If you chose Jesus, it's time to join the love riot.

But before you move on, listen carefully. This is not the gospel reshaped. This is not Christianity diluted. It's not a "teen version" of God or something that's easier to swallow or less life altering.

Following God *does* change your life. This is your call to let Him.

— Going Deeper —

1. What's your reaction to the "free money" shopping event story? How would you have spent your fifty dollars?

2. I talk about apathy and complacency a lot in this chapter. How do you define those two words? How do you think they've shown up in your life?

3. Even though our lives can often be very "Christianized," why do you think we are lacking passion and commitment to God?

4. What do phrases like "wholehearted commitment" and "radical devotion" mean to you? Do you think God is asking that of us? How can we practically follow Him?

5. Which choice did you make at the end of this chapter? How can you apply that choice today?

2

it's not just a pizza party

God's a lot bigger and so is the church

All around me, people were singing and lifting their hands, worshiping Jesus.

I was trying to worship too. Really, I was. But this particular Sunday, it wasn't coming easily. My heart wasn't in it. I mouthed the words to the songs, feeling a little like a hypocrite. I tried lifting my hands. It felt hollow. Insincere.

It had been a hard week, and my faith tank was running on empty. I *wanted* to want to be in church. I *wanted* to want to worship. But I didn't. Instead I wished I was anywhere but in church, trying to dredge up worship from my worshipless heart.

I glanced at the people standing in the aisles nearby. I was always the girl people came up to after the service to say things like, "I just love to watch you sing and praise Jesus. You have such a fire for God."

Well, today I hoped they weren't watching because that fire was burning low.

This wasn't the first time though. I'd felt this lowness before—in church during worship or at home during my prayer and Bible time. The penchant toward apathy. The longing for comfort, familiarity, and entertainment. The fear of being radically sold out for Christ.

And what's more, I knew I wasn't the only one who felt this way. I'd watched my friends and peers battling the same longings and fears, giving in to the lukewarm. Inside my heart was one loud cry of *Why?* followed by *How?* Why do we lose passion for Christ? Why does the fire die? How do we—enthusiastic, energetic teenagers—seem to have enthusiasm and energy for so many other things except Jesus?

While I could list dozens of reasons we experience complacency in our faith, I want to focus on what I believe is the biggest one: the fact that we greatly underestimate two things—God and the church.

Who Is God *Really*?

Is it really possible to underestimate God?

You bet.

In fact, it's not only possible, it's actually impossible *not* to underestimate Him. Our human minds can only comprehend so much, and there are things about God that we'll never be able to completely understand. However, if we want to be passionately in love with Him, we have to know who He is, even if His true depth is incomprehensible. If we don't know who God is, we won't know how to live for Him.

God Is Elohim (Our Creator)

I'm sure you've heard this before, but it deserves to be repeated. *God created us out of the dust of the earth.* The dust that He also created, by the way.

Elohim is one of the many names of God. It implies His strength and power, and it's also the first name for God found in the Bible. Right in Genesis 1:1, it tells us: "In the beginning God [*Elohim*] created the heavens and the earth." Every single part of the universe—from billions of galaxies to the most majestic mountains, from the hair on your head to the atoms and molecules that comprise it all—was designed and created by God. He spoke and light sprang forth. He spoke and the planets were born into being. He spoke and every plant, great and small, flourished. He spoke and every animal, bird, insect, and fish awakened into existence, breath filling lungs and hearts beginning to beat.

As I look at the world, I see in it aspects of *Elohim*. Creation bearing the image of its Creator. I've heard it said that the beauty of God's creation is only a twinkling star in the blazing sun of His glory. Extraordinary doesn't begin to describe it, and I don't have words that can either. As I imagine God lovingly creating a people that would rebel against Him, a world that would turn from Him, I can't imagine why He would continue His work of art, except for the simple fact that He *loved* it.

God Is Savior (Our Redeemer)

Because of our rebellion against God's perfect plan, our relationship with Him shattered. But God still loved us enough that He continued to forgive as thousands of years went by. During this time, a complex and rigorous system was put in place. Only a few specific people were able to enter into God's holy presence, and everyone was required to offer animal sacrifices to cover their sins. It was a demanding system that clearly showed the brokenness of the relationship between God and humankind. Not very sustainable, to say the least. But God had a better plan in mind—a Savior to bring an end to the old ways, become the final sacrifice, redeem us, and usher in a new system. So God became flesh on earth as a baby named Jesus who lived among us and eventually died by our hands *for us*.

I have to confess that my heart is more hardened to this story than I'd like to admit. Yours probably is too. It's easy to think, *Yeah, yeah, I know all this*, because we know the facts—we know what happened, how it happened, and all that. However, when I've struggled to understand the magnitude of Christ's sacrifice, God has been gracious to gently remind me that, even in the middle of knowing it, I've still forgotten. Let's remember together.

Our sin sent Jesus to the cross and held Him there until He cried out, "It is finished" (John 19:30). Imagine the stripes laid across His back, the nails that pierced His hands, His agony at being separated from God the Father. And keep in mind that He endured it all for you. He loves you that much. C. S. Lewis said, "When Christ died, He died for you individually just as much as if you'd been the only man in the world."[1] He willingly placed Himself upon the altar and became at the same time, priest and sacrifice, victor and victim.

Then He conquered death, making our salvation complete, if only we accept it and turn to Him. He died because of His intense love for us and His desire to know us intimately. I'm praying we grasp the beauty of this. That *love*. That *sacrifice*. It's unimaginable, but it's our story.

God Is Abba (Our Father)

Out of all the names and characteristics of God, this is my favorite. Out of His power, He created us. Out of His sacrifice, He saved us. But out of His gentle love, He promises that He's also our *Abba*—literally our daddy.

In Isaiah 49, God asks, "Can a mother forget . . . the child she has borne?" His answer? "Though she may forget, I will not forget you! See, I have engraved you on the palms of my hands" (vv. 15–16 NIV). God's saying that, as strong as a mother's love may be,

His love is even stronger. Our names are engraved on the palms of His hands and forever written on His heart. Though we may forget Him, He never forgets us.

God Is Holy and Worthy of Our Praise

In the book of Revelation, we get a glimpse of an extremely dramatic scene—more dramatic, high-tension, and awe-inspiring than anything we could ever fathom. We get to take a step into the throne room of God and get a brief description of who He is. Featured in this scene are four creatures, who seem a little terrifying and like they might fit into a sci-fi thriller—who said the Bible was boring? They don't rest day or night from saying one phrase over and over again: *"Holy, holy, holy, Lord God Almighty"* (Rev. 4:8, italics added). They're ceaseless in their praise, because no matter how many times we praise Him or what kind of words we use, we'll never be able to come close to matching our holy, perfect, all-powerful God.

God Is So Much More

As we move forward in this book, I pray you seek God for yourself. I'm warning you though, the more you learn about God, the more you'll realize there's so much more to know. Some of it we'll discover, but a lot of it we won't know until we reach heaven. He's more powerful than we can imagine, more loving than we can grasp. But that shouldn't stop us from seeking Him. I challenge you to cry out to God like Moses did: "Show me Your glory" (Exod. 33:18). He will, but once you taste it, it'll never be enough—you'll always long for more.[2]

What—or Who—Is the Church?

God is the biggest and most important part in this story, but there's another character on the stage. And that's the church.

There are a lot of misconceptions about what the church is. Contrary to what many people think, the church isn't a "what" at all, but rather a "who."

It's us. God designed the church to be a worldwide body of believers that pushes and encourages us in our walk with Him. That's why we go to a church—because we are *the* church. It's a place where we can learn, grow, serve, and spend time with other Christians. It's important to be connected to the worldwide church by being a part of a local church, because that's where we're able to learn from our spiritual "family," serve others, and grow closer to Jesus. We can't fly solo in our relationship with God or have an isolated faith. We need other people. We need the church. And the church needs us.

Let's dig deep and learn what the church is *not*.

The Church Is Not a Denomination

A few years ago, an older woman I didn't know approached me and asked, "What denomination are you?" Apparently, I not only looked like someone who would know what the word *denomination* means but would also be a part of one. I stared at her for a few seconds, taken off guard, my mind reeling as I tried to think of an answer.

Well, my parents used to attend a Methodist church when I was a baby, then we went to a Baptist church. I also went to a home church for a few years, and now I'm at a nondenominational church. What would that make me? I've never really thought about it . . .

Eventually, I mumbled the name of the church my family and I attend, but in the back of my mind I was really thinking, *Umm . . . I'm just a Christian.* Smooth, Sara, real smooth. Do I get points for awkwardness?

While I hope I could answer that question now with a bit more poise, I still consider myself "just a Christian." I believe in the Bible. It's God's complete and flawless Word, filled with absolute truth and not even one error. Denominational differences exist, but they're often surface issues. Scripture is the bottom line. It's what brings unity to the worldwide church, because it's what really matters. It's true, however, that even Scripture interpretations vary, so we need to continually dig into the Word ourselves and use the wisdom and discernment provided by the Holy Spirit.

A church should draw us closer to Jesus, teach us Scripture, challenge us to dig into it ourselves, equip us to go out and serve and share the gospel, and be a place where we're always learning, growing, giving, and receiving. Sadly, in a world of compromise, we sometimes find churches of compromise. Just because a building is supposed to be a church doesn't mean it's a solid example of one. This is why we have to be wise, discerning, and always go back to that bottom line: *Does everything agree with the Bible?* A difference in worship and style isn't the most important thing but, rather, how strong and uncompromising their foundation of Scripture is and their stance on living and teaching the gospel.

The Church Is Not a Building

It's easy to think of church as a building or a structure that God blesses because of its name. But that's actually not the case. The building is merely where we gather—it's not what makes the church.

Church can be anywhere. It can be in a field. It can take place in a dungeon or prison cell where people persecuted for Christ worship Him anyway. The church can meet in the aisles of Walmart during an impromptu prayer meeting. It can be in a home. The church can be anywhere, because Jesus tells us that "where two or three are gathered together in My name, I am there in the midst of them" (Matt. 18:20). The Holy Spirit doesn't live in a building—He lives in our hearts. So wherever we go, He comes with us, be it to church or the mall.

That doesn't mean we can or should skip out on attending a church. Scripture tells us that going to church and meeting with other believers regularly is a vital aspect of being a Christian (see Heb. 10:25). Because when a group of Jesus-loving people come together, God is in the midst of them.

The Church Is Not for Perfect People

Jesus said it best. "It is not the healthy who need a doctor, but the sick" (Matt. 9:12 NIV). Some people approach church and Christianity with an "I need to get my act together first" attitude, but if we wait until we're perfect before we come to Jesus, we're going to be waiting a long time. A mother once told me that her children had stopped coming to church because they felt they weren't worthy to be there after all they'd done. If our pasts and our sins can keep us out of the church, they can keep us away from God. It's only by coming to God that we can be free from the burden of a life without Him.

Jesus died to cover our imperfections with His spotless sacrifice, take our righteousness—the equivalent of filthy rags (see Isa. 64:6)—and make us whiter than snow. The church isn't made up of perfect people but forgiven people.

The Church Is Not about Entertainment

I've noticed a new trend in churches. Because they've heard the gloomy message that Generation Z is leaving them in the dust, churches are finding creative ways to keep us within their walls. Pizza parties? Okay, how about one a month? Small groups? We're on it. Ping-pong matches? What about softball? Or how about an escape room? Check, check, check. Ugly Christmas sweater parties, turkey bowling, and color wars at the park? Sure thing.

Of course, we love it. And why not? These are all fun activities. (I don't know about you, but I think escape rooms are seriously awesome!) And they *do* draw us in. We even bring our unchurched friends and we all have a blast. But when the last pizza box is thrown away and our ugly sweater is packed up for next year, what did we gain? We probably heard a message and sang a few songs, but it was like the opening band at a concert. Who came for them? We're here for the headliner. We're given a nugget of truth surrounded with layers of fluff. On the church scales, it seems like outreach trumps discipleship, but both need a place. Outreach is important, but serious discipleship is vital for spiritual growth.

Truth be told, it's not solely the church's fault. Churches can have pizza parties if they want—they're not the root of the problem. The real problem is that too many people approach God and the church with a pizza-party mentality. They ask, "What can I gain?" instead of "What can I give?"; "How much fun can I have?" instead of "How can I learn, grow, and serve?"

What both the world and the church need is a generation of young people who will turn this perspective upside down. Who will boldly and passionately declare: "I don't need a pizza party to keep me in church—I need Jesus. I need the gospel. I need challenge and conviction. And I'm willing to go all the way for Christ."

We've laid the foundation. Now let's start moving onward, upward, and inward.

Do you hear Him calling? Are you daring enough to listen?

— Going Deeper —

1. Have you found that when it comes to God, you experience a "penchant toward apathy" and a "fear of being radically sold out for Christ"? Why do you think that is?

2. What is your favorite aspect of God's character and which one do you think you underestimate the most?

3. Did any of the aspects of God's character surprise you? What would you add to the list?

4. Do you tend to think of the church as a denomination or a building? Does this chapter alter the way you think about it? How?

5. In your own experience, do you find that church is often about entertainment? How can you help change that?

i don't want a facebook Jesus

let's go beyond the surface

Outwardly, Bella is a model of the perfect Christian girl. Raised in a Christian family, she goes to church every Sunday and youth group every Wednesday. She volunteers at local ministries and leads a small group at Bible camp each year. You'd never consider her to be wild, rebellious, or even wayward.

But get to know her, and you'll find a girl hurting and struggling, trying to walk a tightrope between God and the world. Pulled in two different directions, Bella's struggles reflect the emptiness and searching we all experience without Christ—even though she's been surrounded with religion her entire life.

Meghan is the same way, except that, unlike Bella, she seems happy. Unfortunately, that's also just a cover-up. Her parents are worried about her, her friends are weak and shallow, and media influences drive her life. Her feel-good philosophy determines what she believes and how she lives.

Both of these girls are Christians. But something is still missing from their lives.

Our Christianity Illusion

It's easy to have a superficial Christianity. And I'm not just talking about Bella and Meghan.

I'm talking about *me*.

I grew up in a Christian family. I know the right things to say and do to make myself look like the picture-perfect Christian. I rock Christian bumper stickers on my car. I'm a great VBS leader (you don't know what a spiritual accomplishment that really is until you have to entertain a dozen three-year-olds for two hours). I have a seriously impressive collection of "witness wear"—T-shirts and jewelry emblazoned with Scripture verses and catchy quotes. It's easy to fall back on these "accomplishments," a good reputation, and all the compliments from people at church. "Oh, you're such a beautiful Christian girl. It's so good to see young people in church."

I've felt the temptation to coast by on my "godly good-girl" reputation and not work on my relationship with Christ.

The truth is that it's easy to create an illusion of Christianity. If you get a Christian T-shirt (make that three or four, and be sure to pick up one from a good Christian musician), post Scripture verses on Facebook and Instagram, go to church every week, attend youth group, know the Christian lingo, and throw in a few volunteer opportunities for good measure, you're all set. Seriously.

The illusion isn't true though. It doesn't have depth, and it can't last. Real Christianity is raw and gritty, full of deep struggles and sincere passion. A list of things we do, and a longer list of things we don't, will never—*can never*—replace an authentic relationship with Christ. It only scratches the surface when what God really wants is our hearts—and what our hearts really need is God. Being a picture-perfect Christian might build our egos, but being a Jesus follower isn't about building our egos but building His kingdom. We can slide by with our cover story, but we're missing the big picture.

The whole thing reminds me of Facebook. Yep, *Facebook*.

I only have a few hundred Facebook friends. Pretty pathetic, I know. But the crazy thing is that I consider myself *good friends* with only about ten of them—two of whom are my mom and sister. The remaining several hundred fall into the categories of casual friends and acquaintances or people who know someone I know. I could probably tell you my relationship with each of them. For some it might be, "We go to the same service at church," others, "They live down the road," and a few, "I have no idea . . ."

But I don't actually *know* them. I might know what kind of ice cream they like or what they did over the weekend, but I don't know their struggles. I don't know their priorities or passions. I don't know their hearts.

And they don't know mine. For many of us, that's what our relationship with Jesus is like.

We have a form of a relationship. We identify enough with Him that we go to church, volunteer, occasionally read the Bible, and send up a prayer when we need help. We think we're a pretty good person and surely that earns us the title of "Christian." We say we know God, but do we really? Does the relationship go any deeper than a superficial Facebook friendship? Jesus won't settle for a half-hearted "like" or even a slightly more enthusiastic "love."

Just like a friendship needs more than an occasional text or like to thrive, so does our relationship with God. It takes work, sacrifice, and time. Many of us (myself included, at times) don't give up time or put in effort to truly seek God. Our complacency in the relationship is defined by the lack of effort we give.

It comes down to the fact that it's easy to be a card-carrying Christian without it really changing our lives.

But Jesus longs for so much more.

You Gotta Know Him

We're not the first generation to fall into this pattern. Way before Facebook was even invented (about two thousand years before, actually), Jesus talked about this very thing.

In Matthew 7, Jesus warns us,

> Not everyone who says to Me, "Lord, Lord," shall enter the kingdom of heaven, but he who does the will of My Father in heaven. Many will say to me in that day, "Lord, Lord, have we not prophesied in Your name, cast out demons in Your name, and done many wonders in Your name?" And then I will declare to them, "I never knew you." (vv. 21–23)

My first impression upon reading that list of accomplishments is, *Wow, they're doing pretty good.* I mean, prophesying and doing wonders? Sounds to me like they're bringing their A game and following Jesus pretty well.

But Jesus is serious. Notice He doesn't tell them, "You didn't do enough for me," "You didn't follow the Christian culture rules enough," or "You didn't look like the model Christian."

He said He didn't *know* them.

The Greek word for "knew" in this passage is *ginōskō.*[1] It covers a wide range of knowledge, including perception, understanding, and figuring out what's true. It also means coming to know through personal, firsthand experience. It's not just head knowledge, or a passed-down knowledge, but a firsthand intimacy brought on by personal experience.

When Jesus said He didn't know them, He was saying He didn't know their hearts, because they'd never surrendered to Him and

His will. They'd never sought Him for the mere sake of knowing Him. They did things for Him but they didn't intimately know Him, and He didn't know them either. Dean Inserra, pastor of City Church, put it this way:

> Jesus wasn't speaking about atheists, agnostics, pluralists, or secular humanists. He was describing moral people doing good religious acts in the name of God. Religion was deeply embedded in their routines, which gave them full confidence that their acts of righteousness set them up for a big payoff in heaven.[2]

In our society, they would probably be the star kid in youth group or the person leading worship. But their actions *for* God and their relationship *with* God were way out of balance.

How like them we are.

Our plea might sound something like this: "Lord, Lord, didn't I go to church every Sunday? Didn't I go on that mission trip with my church? Didn't I fulfill the Bible memorization goal at youth group? Didn't I save sex for marriage? Didn't I refuse to watch R-rated movies? Didn't I do all this stuff? Doesn't it count at all?"

Even people who don't consider themselves Christians could have a pretty good defense: "Lord, Lord, didn't I help the homeless in my city? Didn't I refuse to steal from my company when I had the chance? Didn't I help and encourage my friends? Wasn't I a good person? Wasn't I better than a lot of other people? Don't these things matter at all?"

And maybe after we rattled off our lists, God would sigh and say, "But I didn't know your *heart*. You never gave it to me. You never loved me. Not like I love you."

Author David Platt says,

> When Jesus came on the scene in human history and began calling followers to himself, he did not say, "Follow certain rules.

Observe specific regulations. Perform ritual duties. Pursue a particular path." Instead, he said, "Follow *me*." With these two simple words, Jesus made clear that his primary purpose was not to instruct his disciples in a prescribed religion; his primary purpose was to invite his disciples into a personal relationship. . . . This extremely shocking and utterly revolutionary call is the essence of what it means to be a disciple of Jesus: we are not called to simply believe certain points or observe certain practices, but ultimately to cling to the person of Christ as life itself.[3]

What God wants more than anything—more than our lists and rules and attempts to earn our own salvation—is our love.

Your Love Matters

Throughout the rest of this book, we're going to learn how to follow Jesus, serve Him, embrace radical obedience, awaken complete commitment, and live sold out for Him.

But before you read another word, I need to make one thing clear.

None of it matters if it's not motivated by love.

Did you hear that? Read it again, slowly.

None of it matters if it's not motivated by love.

I don't want to tell you how to be the picture-perfect Christian. I don't want to write a book that leaves you with a to-do list.

I want to share the love that's exploded in my soul, and I want you to experience it as well.

Because, when it comes down to it, love for God is what matters and love for God is what lasts.

Jesus tells us the first and greatest commandment is, "You shall love the LORD your God with all your heart, with all your soul, and with all your mind" (Matt. 22:37). Love is the first commandment, and the first thing we have to understand if we want to live for God. I could write thousands of words trying to persuade you to serve God and not make a dent in your relationship with Him. It's only when you choose to surrender to Jesus and let His love for you spark a love for Him that a desire to serve God and live for Him will matter.

Throughout the years I've been a Christian, I've always felt my love for God is deeply inadequate. Because it is. He deserves more love and worship than I can humanly offer. There are moments when I feel more, and there are times when I struggle to feel anything. But I've learned that my relationship with God can't be motivated by my fickle feelings but rather by my intentional decision to come before God in obedience. Love is a choice, as well as an emotion. And when it comes to God, the choice of love sparks the reality of love. We often elevate emotional love for God over obedient love, overemotionalizing what our love for Him should look like. But our emotions are fickle and constantly changing. If we allow them to dictate our perception of God, it will rarely be the God of the Bible. I've learned to seek Him even when I don't feel like it. I go to His Word, and dive into its truth, letting it wash my soul. I remember how much He loves me and all He offered and sacrificed on my behalf. And I ask for help to love Him more, telling Him I don't always feel it. He already knows and isn't surprised by my weakness. And I've found that this love—one of obedience and seeking hard after God—is more constant than if I waited to seek God until all the "feels" lined up. This is the love I pray for—one that will chase after God no matter what. I believe those honest and vulnerable prayers honor Him. Desperate cries from a weak and finite human heart that is longing to long for His holiness. Looking through old prayer journals, I read my prayers and my heart fills with gratitude for all the ways He's answered them. Not always as I would have liked, but there's one prayer He's never failed to answer: *Help me love You more.* Over the years, I've prayed:

Jesus, I run to You for You're my hiding place. I don't feel like I love You enough. I want to, but I don't always know how. Draw me closer to You.

You, Lord, and only You, can satisfy me. I have experienced the deep well of Your love, yet I still run to others to fill me up. Draw me back to You. I say yes to You, Lord. Yes.

I'm still seeking Him and praying for more love. I don't think I'll ever stop, because I'll never have enough. The more I focus on His love for me, the more I want to love Him. And the more I love Him, the more I seek Him and focus on His love . . . causing a beautiful, never-ending pattern of seeking and finding, pursuing and being pursued.

I've been asked, and I've wondered myself, "How do I fall in love with Jesus?"

The answer isn't complicated, and there's not an in-depth step-by-step program I can point you toward. Boiled down, it's simply this: Surrender to His love. Pursue His presence. Follow and obey Him. Repeat.

He transforms our hearts as we seek Him and surrender to Him. That's what we want—internal transformation instead of external religion. Without the component of this radical, intentional love, our actions are dry and superficial. You can have actions without love, but you can never have true love without actions.

It's Worth It

Does a part of your heart rebel against this? Do you think constantly seeking after God might not be worth it? Or that it's too much work?

I understand. You're not alone. But may I gently ask: Have you ever experienced God's love?

This walk is not easy. Constant pursuit and obedience is not always fun. It's a discipline and one that can be costly. But once you experience His love, you realize it's completely worth it. Without Him, something will always be lacking in your life, and you'll never be fully satisfied.

Try it. I challenge you to ask God for more of Himself and see if He doesn't answer.

Remember when I said something was still missing in Bella and Meghan's lives?

It was love for God. Pure, undivided love that draws you to a relationship deeper than the T-shirt you wear, the songs you listen to, and the rules you follow and things you avoid.

If I could sit down and share my heart with you and those girls, this is what I'd say: He's worth it. God's love is deep and wide and everything you could ever ask for. It satisfies your soul and makes you hungry for more. It spurs you on to action and starts a fire in your soul to serve Him with everything in you.

Are you ready to experience God in a whole, new way? Do you want to learn more about Him? Do you want to *know* Him? Really, truly know Him?

Today, ask Him for more of Himself. Obediently seek Him through Scripture, and ask Him to help you love Him more.

He *always* answers that prayer.

I don't know about you, but I want so much more than just a Facebook Jesus.

— Going Deeper —

1. Do you know someone like Bella or Meghan? What do you notice in their lives? Do you see any of the same qualities in yourself?

2. What superficial actions have you embraced to make yourself feel a connection with God?

3. What's one practical way you can surrender to God's love today (e.g., spend time reading the Bible or praying)? Do it before the day is over.

4. Does your heart rebel against the thought of fully pursuing God? Why? Follow through on the challenge and ask God for a greater love for Him.

5. I want to leave you with one of my favorite quotes that's turned into a prayer I repeat over and over. A. W. Tozer says in his book *The Pursuit of God*:

> O God, I have tasted Thy goodness, and it has both satisfied me and made me thirsty for more. I am painfully conscious of my need for further grace. I am ashamed of my lack of desire. O God, the Triune God, I want to want Thee; I long to be filled with longing; I thirst to be made more thirsty still. Show me Thy glory, I pray Thee, so that I may know Thee indeed. Begin in mercy a new work of love within me. Say to my soul "Rise up my love, my fair one, and come away." Then give me grace to rise and follow Thee up from this misty lowland where I have wandered so long.[4]

What stands out to you in this prayer? Be bold enough to pray it, and ask that God would help you fall more in love with Him.

PART TWO

the change

4

get ready for a renovation

he'll flip your life

Have you ever watched those HGTV home renovation shows? You know, the kind where they take an old, rundown house and turn it into a beautiful, trendy home? The renovation can be so drastic, sometimes you don't even recognize the before and after.

I've never really been a fan of those shows. Maybe because the idea of watching someone else work is exhausting, or maybe because it's a little too close to my real life. My family and I almost literally flipped the house we're living in now. From lifting it up and building a basement underneath—I'm totally serious—painting over the horrendous orange that covered the walls, pulling out the strange, metal staircase, and ripping up floorboards, we did a major remodel. By the end of it, I felt like I was living a personal version of *Fixer Upper*—with the added bonus of sore muscles, late nights, and endless visits to the home improvement store.

Never. Again.

Despite my personal dislike of house renovations, I will admit that the outcome is always beautiful. I have the deepest respect for people who have the ability to see something as it *could be* instead of merely seeing *what is*.

Spiritually speaking, we're a lot like those rundown buildings, aren't we? On our own, we're not very impressive. In fact, we can be broken-down and dirty. Our foundation is unsteady, wiring all messed up, and termites and cockroaches live in the corners where we think no one looks. We desperately need a renovation. Something new and fresh. Something to clean up the ugly parts inside and fix what's falling apart.

Good for us, because what HGTV does to houses, God does to souls. He sees what *could be* instead of *what is*. He sees all our problems and issues, but He has a better vision for our lives.

He radically, beautifully renovates us with His love. In this chapter, I'm going to show you what that looks like. But first, meet Anna—a girl God drastically transformed.

From Atheist to Jesus Follower

"I was an atheist for five years, and not a passive one."

That's how nineteen-year-old Anna described herself. After leaving her childhood church—a place of rules and rituals—she poured herself into researching anything and everything to disprove Christianity. "I was an enemy of God's kingdom and didn't give it a second thought," she remembers.

This was working fine—until her junior year of high school. An eating disorder and one breakup later, Anna hit rock bottom. Heartbroken, self-image destroyed, her mind was in turmoil, her life and relationships a mess. Desperate, she tried out one solution after another, chasing after the promises of happiness and healing they offered. They all came up empty and she was left feeling more drained and hopeless than before.

"I was ready to give up and just resign myself to never finding what my heart was thirsting for. I had no way to dig myself out of the hole I had dug, and for the first time I gave suicide more than a moment's thought."

But then God showed up.

One summer, He brought a girl named Kristen into Anna's life. Kristen was kind, sweet, funny, caring—and a Christian. Anna didn't understand how Kristen could enjoy spending time with her, because every time they were together, Anna made it clear she was antagonistic toward Kristen's faith, questioning her frequently and bringing up every argument she could imagine. "But whenever I confronted her, she never stopped defending this God of hers. She didn't act confused or as though she was having second thoughts. It was perplexing but . . . intriguing."

Kristen and her family continued to reach out and love Anna. They spoke freely of their faith even though she was adamantly opposed to it. Little by little, Anna's defenses crumbled, and she began to realize her arguments against Christianity didn't add up.

Curious, she decided to discover God for herself. She picked up the Bible that had been collecting dust on her bookshelf for years and started reading in the book of Ecclesiastes. Outlined there was a path she'd personally taken—one where she tried everything and it all came up lacking. She knew that feeling well. Now she knew God had an answer for it—Himself. She kept reading. When she reached the Gospel of John, the remaining shell around her heart cracked as she read about a Savior perfectly good and loving. Anna later wrote, "I saw a man die a horrific death for the people He loved. And I knew Jesus Christ was my Savior. I knew He was the One I'd been looking for my whole life. I fell into open arms." After that, everything changed for Anna.

> My dreams and plans changed, the way I managed my time, when I got up, how I organized my day, where I went at night, what I did in the evenings, who I hung out with, what I said, how I served

my family, how I approached people, how I dressed, how often I went to church, how I did my work, the kind of work I did, what I listened to, what I watched, how I saw my career, all my morals, my values, my innermost desires all changed. *Everything.*

God healed Anna that summer. She wrote in her testimony,

He flooded the deepest crevices of my heart with warmth, forgiveness, and love. He healed scars I didn't know I had. He healed years of hurt, loneliness, anger, and insecurity. I'd known passion and lust and laughter, but never a joy so deep and rich—a joy that brings tears to my eyes, ready to burst with the happiness inside, a joy that turned my life upside down and changed every aspect of how I live. It was real joy. It was *love.*

That's our God. Our transforming, loving, all-powerful God. He took an atheist and turned her into one of the most passionate Jesus followers I know. He heals us and makes us new. And once God captures our hearts, we're never the same again.

Flipped Heart, Flipped Life

You don't have to start out as an atheist for God to change you.

God's changed me. Even though I don't have a grand conversion story and have considered myself a Christian since the age of five, I still know He's changed me. I think differently, talk differently, and have different priorities. I look at the world and it's not like me, and I'm not like it. I don't say this to brag or make myself sound perfect—I'm far from it. God's led me on a different kind of transformative journey. One where, instead of looking back and seeing who I was, I look back and see who I might have been. Without Jesus, I know my life story would look entirely different.

No matter your story, the fact remains that you can't wholeheartedly love Christ and stay the same. When you love someone, it changes everything.

When you sincerely love God, you have new purpose a
Even things as small as whom you hang out with, wha
music you listen to, and what you do in your free time alters.
Why? Because you've fallen in love and want to please the one
you love.

These changes are external, but genuine external change is a
product of genuine internal change. Anyone can find a new set
of friends or switch out their music playlist, but if we put all the
emphasis on external changes without realizing that they're a
natural consequence of a changed heart, we're way out of balance. That's when legalism and a works-based religion occur.
It's impossible to force internal change. Something has to be the
catalyst. For Christ followers, that catalyst is our love for God.

Insecurities, priorities, thought processes, life goals, what we
spend our time on, and the things we love are products of our
heart. If our heart isn't changed, nothing else changes either.
But if our heart is changed by love for God, these, and so many
other areas, are altered. Once your heart is changed, your entire
life gets a makeover.

Let God Dig Deep

I can't tell you exactly what needs to be altered in your life. It's
different for everyone, but certain things are universal. Like our
thoughts. Controlling what we let in our minds is a battle for
everyone. I know it is for me. What I think about matters to
God, because He says that lust equals adultery and hatred equals
murder, and He challenges us to think of things that are true,
noble, and pure. He wants us to take every thought captive (see
Matt. 5:27–30, 1 John 3:15, Phil. 4:8, and 2 Cor. 10:4–6).

I also know He wants to change the way we talk. Hurtful
words, cursing, lying, negativity, and sarcastic remarks are just
a few of the things that regularly come out of our mouths without
even thinking about it. But God tells us that life and death are

in the power of the tongue and to speak words that are good, pure, and edifying (see Prov. 18:21, Eph. 4:29, and James 3:1–12).

Relationships are another thing that change drastically when we place them under God's control. From how we respect our parents and those in authority (like our teachers, employers, and government officials) to how we respond to the opposite sex. Relationships handled God's way look extremely different from how the world around us operates. In a society that takes God's plan for sex casually, we're called to value purity and save sex for marriage. When our peers are rebelling against authority, we're called to respect those placed over us through the way we talk to and about them.

God tells us that we'll know Christians by the fruit in their lives, by the way we speak, act, and relate to those around us. We walk and live differently because we're following a different standard— one that can't be found in the latest Hollywood hit or in our culture at large, but one that's outlined clearly in the Word of God (see Eph. 4:21–32). God's way is one of purity, integrity, humility, and love. Changes like these are the evidence—the fruit—of a heart transformed by salvation and love for God. The "master change" of salvation is the catalyst for every subsequent change.

What needs to be renovated in your life? If you're wondering how you'll know what needs to be changed, all you have to do is ask Him and search His Word. Psalm 139 demonstrates this when the psalmist said, "Search me, O God, and know my heart; try me, and know my anxieties; and see if there is any wicked way in me" (vv. 23–24).

God knows us better than we know ourselves. He sees the parts of our hearts and lives we try to keep hidden from others, or even from ourselves, and those are the places He especially wants to work on. Psalm 19:12–14 says, "Cleanse me from secret faults . . . Let the words of my mouth and the meditation of my heart be acceptable in your sight, O Lord, my strength and my Redeemer."

Intentionally invite God to search your heart and life to reveal areas that need to be remade. Believe me, He will. I remember one morning when I prayed the words of Psalm 139. I didn't expect that He'd actually answer, but it only took about an hour before He'd convicted me about the unbiblical thought patterns and pride in my heart. *Ouch!* And this wasn't the only occasion, by any means. From the way I relate to my parents and sister to entertainment choices that aren't edifying to how I speak about others, God is constantly revealing areas in my life that need to be changed.

As He brings things to the surface, it won't be easy, but as we're remodeled and renewed, we grow closer to Him and become a clearer picture of who He is. He often brings problems to our attention through time spent with Him, as we pray and dig into His Word. He sometimes leads us toward change through the guidance of other people. It hurts to have someone tell us what's out of line in our lives, but it can be extremely helpful to view ourselves through another person's perspective.

Our God is a practical, hands-on God. He wants even the nitty-gritty parts of our lives to reflect Him. Let Him dig deep and follow through on the process of change—even if it's uncomfortable.

Don't Settle for an Incomplete Renovation

If we're completely honest, the biggest reason we resist change is because we're comfortable with ourselves.

I'm comfortable with me. With my little sins and tiny rebellions. The things no one knows about that don't seem very bad. I sometimes find myself thinking, *I mean, it's just a bit of pride. Just a self-centered thought or unkind word.*

This is where it gets real. Many people claim to be Christians but still live exactly like non-Christians. There's no evidence of a changed heart or changed life in their actions, attitudes, relationships, or speech. Why? Because their former lives—former selves—don't seem that bad. Because they're comfortable and familiar. *C'mon*, we think, *change in the big areas is enough. Surely just being saved is enough. God can't really expect us to alter our lives that much, can He?*

But you see, God doesn't change for us. We change for Him. He doesn't alter His standards to fit into our lifestyle. We alter our lifestyle to live out His standards and become a reflection of His perfection.

Remember the illustration I used of renovating a house? It applies here too. Not allowing God to dig deep and change even those secret, "not too bad" parts is like an incomplete renovation. Just getting saved means the ownership of the house has been transferred to God's name. But there's still a lot of work that needs to be done.

I love the illustration C. S. Lewis created in his book *Mere Christianity*. He defined how God remodels our lives, also using the analogy of a house renovation to describe how He doesn't just come to clean out the mess, but instead comes to transform us entirely. Lewis wrote, "You thought you were going to be made into a decent little cottage: but He is building a palace. He intends to come and live in it Himself."[1]

God has a greater vision for us than we have for ourselves. His ultimate goal is to form us into the image of Christ. Until that happens (and that doesn't fully happen until Heaven), He keeps working. We are far too easily satisfied with our incomplete transformation, because we don't see what He sees. He sees what could be and He will settle for nothing less. So in the meantime, as painful as it may be, He keeps messing with our old ways and habits.

Pride—torn down. Selfishness and self-focus—ripped away. Envy, jealousy, bitterness—chiseled off. Impure thoughts—destroyed. Anger—crushed. Lust—shattered.

With each change, God goes deeper, removing what's dirty and replacing it with His cleanness. We start to look less like us and more like Him—pure, loving, gracious, kind. We bear the indelible image of our renovator and become testimonies of His grace. That's why He's persistent in perfecting us. Our changed life is a lighthouse shining God's love for all to see. Well-known evangelist Billy Graham once said, "Being a Christian is more than just an instantaneous conversion—it is a daily process whereby you grow to be more and more like Christ."[2]

From Rebel to Missionary

Only God could turn a die-hard thief and liar who had self-professed "wicked behavior" and an "unrepentant spirit"[3] into a missionary.

But that's exactly what He did for George Müller.

By the age of ten, George was stealing money from his own father. By the age of fourteen, he'd progressed to gambling with friends and getting drunk regularly.

But God still had plans for George. In 1825, when he was twenty, a friend invited him to a prayer meeting and that night, everything changed. He later said, "I have no doubt . . . that He began a work of grace in me. Even though I scarcely had any knowledge of who God truly was, that evening was the turning point in my life."[4]

What a turning point it was! George gave up drinking, gambling, lying, and stealing, and decided to become a missionary. He opened orphanages and cared for over ten thousand children throughout his many years of service. He established 117 Christian schools, which allowed over 120,000 children to get an education. But perhaps the most impressive thing about this man was that he never asked for financial help—he simply prayed and God answered. Whether he prayed for God to provide breakfast for the orphans when there wasn't any food in the house, for financial provision, or even just for God to change the weather hindering him from preaching somewhere, his faith never wavered.

He once said, "I have known my Lord for more than fifty years and there is not one instance that I have failed to have an audience with the King."[5] His life impacted thousands and his testimony and works continue to challenge and encourage people today.

Over and over, God has done transformative works in the lives of His followers. Countless individuals have been drastically changed when they met Christ.

From the atheist determined to disprove Christianity to the young woman grappling with identity.

From the teen caught up in destructive cycles to the older man finally finding peace on his deathbed.

The God we serve is a master at changing our lives, flipping our perspectives, giving us hope, and loving us relentlessly . . . no matter what we've done. He meets us where we are and says we're never too far gone. He turns a mess into a message, a failure into a conqueror, an outcast into a child of God. He transformed Paul, a persecutor of Christians, into a leader of the New Testament church. He took the Samaritan woman, the outcast of society, and made her a testifier of Christ. He gave the woman caught in adultery new life and new hope when He forgave her and said to go and sin no more.

He makes beauty out of brokenness and wholeness out of shattered pieces. He changes the way we live, because we're not of this world and we have a higher calling—to be image bearers of Christ.

Are you willing to let Him work in you? To let Him flip your perspective and way of life? To let Him change you, even if it's hard?

We're all fixer uppers. HGTV flips houses; God flips lives.

People like Anna and George. People like you and me.

The only question is, are you ready for a renovation?

— Going Deeper —

1. Could you relate to the house renovation analogy? What parts of your life are "broken down and dirty" and in need of a renovation?

2. Could you relate to Anna's and George's stories? Which part of their stories struck you the most?

3. How do you think God can change you and the broken-down parts of your life? Have you ever believed that you're too far gone? Do you believe that now? Why?

4. Look back in your life. Can you pinpoint any areas that God has transformed? If yes, what are they and how did that change come about?

5. Are you willing to let God come in and transform your life? Invite Him to do so right now.

5

free wi-fi not included

laying down your comfort zones

The double doors slammed shut behind her. Amanda drew in a deep, shaky breath, then followed the guard down the dingy hallway. Not many sixteen-year-olds willingly choose to go behind jail doors.

But not many sixteen-year-olds have the reason my sister did.

Our mom had started a ministry for women in the local correctional facility a few months earlier. She went with a few other women from our church to minister and share the gospel with the inmates. They gave lessons from Scripture, showed Christian movies, passed out Bibles, and prayed with the women.

Amanda felt drawn to join them as the weeks passed. She wanted to meet these women God was pursuing and be a part of the story unfolding behind jail walls.

She knew it wasn't going to be easy.

As the day drew near for her to join them the first time, questions rattled inside her mind.

What's it going to be like? How will the inmates receive me—a teenager? What about the guards?

Walking down that hallway, she entered a different world. A world without freedom, where even the most ordinary items are sought after and hoarded. A world cut off from family, friends, and everything familiar, where orange uniforms are the going style and privacy is nonexistent. A world that desperately needs Jesus.

That's why my sister entered that world.

But it was still hard. Spiritual attacks before each meeting made it difficult and painful. Being searched by the guards every time they went in and out made it awkward and uncomfortable. Not seeing any real results in the women's lives made it discouraging.

Amanda's comfort zone seemed miles away.

So far throughout this book, we've talked about falling in love with Jesus and letting Him change our lives. In this chapter, we're going to break down how to follow Jesus even when it's uncomfortable.

Because love sometimes takes you into hard places.

Discomfort Aversion

Our world is not very interested in discomfort. Think about it. From commercials advertising the latest and greatest invention destined to transform our lives to the free Wi-Fi available at every restaurant and mall, we're a culture that seeks ease and comfort. I mean, seriously, what would we do without free Wi-Fi?

These small inclinations toward ease show us a lot about how we approach the bigger issues of life. We don't naturally choose the road that presents the most difficulty but rather the one that looks well-traveled and familiar. Peer pressure and expectations play into this. Why do something different when we can blend in and do what everyone else is doing? Why choose something hard when an easy option is available? Why be uncomfortable when we don't have to be?

I totally understand this feeling. Doing different and scary things is extremely difficult for me. I'd much rather stay in my little circle of comfort where everything is familiar and cozy. I can't tell you how many times I've felt sick with fear and anxiety over something I knew I needed to do but really didn't want to do. Big things . . . small things . . . it didn't matter. If it didn't fit inside my comfort zone, I wanted nothing to do with it.

But every time I listened to God and stepped into an uncomfortable situation (I'll admit, a few times I've chickened out) I discovered something beautiful outside my comfort zone. As I looked my fears in the face, I grew bolder and braver.

Most importantly, I knew God was strengthening me for the tasks ahead. I knew He understood how hard certain things were for me, and He graciously gave me the strength to do them. I've grown closer to Jesus outside my comfort zone more than I ever have inside it.

And that's what really matters.

I've learned my comfort zones may feel safe, but in reality, they're a prison keeping me from fully following Christ. I regret so many moments when I said no to God when He asked me to do something difficult. I wonder about the impact those times could have held, if only I'd said yes and followed through, scared or not. There have been times when I've compromised because it felt easier to go with the flow, and I wonder what kind of example I could have set if I'd been bold enough to be different.

I want to be done with regret and compromise. Even if it means being scared and uncomfortable. Following Jesus *will* mean being uncomfortable. But I believe with all my heart it'll be worth it.

I'm praying right now that God gives us the courage to follow Him no matter how uncomfortable it is. Jesus never said following Him would be comfort-zone compatible. He just said He'd be with us.

Four Uncomfortable Things We'll Face

Everyone has a different kind of comfort zone and a different level of brave. We're all unique in our strengths and weaknesses, and what's easy for some could be petrifying for others. Don't feel inferior if you find seemingly small things terrifying. And don't feel superior if you find hard or intimidating things easy. Bravery isn't one size fits all.

No matter what you find difficult or easy, there are four uncomfortable things we'll all face. The details may vary, but the principles and motivation stay the same. Let's dig into the different uncomfortable situations God may call us to and then get practical on how to press on even when we're scared.

1. Countercultural = Counter Comfortable

As followers of God, we're not meant to walk in sync with the world. What the world applauds and approves of without question, we can't accept. Things like abortion, premarital sex, bullying, unclean speech, addictions, lust, and pornography all go directly against His nature.

Jesus flips the way the world works and turns our thinking upside down. We no longer fit into the world, because we're no longer of the world. In their book *Jesus Freaks*, the rock trio DC Talk said,

> From the beginnings of His public ministry, Jesus set the record straight: "*I have come to change the world.*" He had come to change people's thinking. He had come to revolutionize their paradigm— the way they saw the world and had comfortably settled into it, following their own desires, ignoring those around them who needed help, and figuring that was the way to do it because everyone else was doing pretty much the same thing . . . Jesus came to comfort the afflicted, but He also came to afflict the comfortable.[1]

Living a countercultural life is an absolute guarantee for discomfort. Going against the flow is never easy. Driving against traffic is never safe. Holding different beliefs in a liberal society, standing for truth when counterfeits are accepted, choosing love when everyone else is bowing to hate, and fighting for the truth of the gospel isn't comfortable.

But you can't claim to love Jesus and continue in the patterns of the world. It's impossible to fit in when the things driving your life call you to stand out and, sometimes, stand alone.

2. Standing Apart

Excitement buzzed through the air over the release of an upcoming movie. The book it was based on was wildly popular (especially among teen girls), and though I'd never read it, my friend Taylor raved about it. "It's my absolute favorite," she gushed one day when she was hanging out at my house. "You *have* to read it! I can't wait for the movie!" She pulled up the movie trailer on her phone. It did look good. Really good.

We made plans to see it together with my sister, Amanda, and a few other girls when it finally came to our local theater. I couldn't wait. A girls' date with a good movie and pizza after—it can't get much better than that, right?

All our plans shattered one afternoon a few days before the scheduled outing. My sister came home from work with grim news—she'd researched the movie and book during her break and discovered disturbing plot points and overt agendas that completely clashed with our biblical convictions.

Now we had a choice to make. Should we wriggle out of our commitment by coming up with a good excuse? Or tell the truth and share why we didn't feel comfortable watching it?

We eventually decided on the latter. We called Taylor and explained our reasons why we wouldn't be watching the movie. Talk about one awkward phone call.

Our relationship with her was never the same again. Amanda and I tried to stay in touch and didn't act any differently toward her, but little by little, Taylor drifted away.

Standing apart is hard—even with something as small as a movie. It takes grit, determination, and confidence in your convictions to stay strong when everyone else is crumbling under pressure.

And sometimes, standing apart means standing alone. For the high schooler who stood at the flagpole by himself during the annual see you at the pole day, it meant that literally. When no one else showed up, Hayden thought he'd simply wait and pray until others arrived. When no one else arrived, his prayer turned to, *God, as people drive by, let them wonder, let their hearts be pricked. Do something with my standing alone.* It took courage for him not to walk away, to stand out and stand apart, and faithfully pray. But he remained strong.[2]

No matter the situation, standing apart comes with a cost. You might lose friends. You might be mocked and shamed. You might feel uncomfortable. Your family may not understand, and your friends and coworkers may call you unkind names.

You'll rarely have people's applause for standing up for your beliefs. But you may gain their respect and set an example for others to follow. The reason the pull of peer pressure is so strong is because it's seldom broken. There may be others who feel the same way but don't know how to break the mold. Once you stand up, others may follow, but even if they don't, you can know God is pleased with your obedience.

Yes, it may get pretty awkward and uncomfortable when all your friends compromise and watch that movie, go to that party, disobey their parents, bully the new kid, and *you don't.* But it's in these small choices that growth takes place, and it's worth each uncomfortable moment. Because you never know what you may need to stand up for in the future, and it could be a whole lot bigger than not watching a movie.

3. Choosing Integrity

I once heard integrity described as having your secret, private, and public lives align. In other words, not living a double life, acting one way when people are watching but doing a 180-degree flip when you're alone.

Integrity leads you to tell the truth, even if the truth paints you in a bad light. It nudges you to speak up, even when staying quiet could protect your reputation and comfort. Living out integrity day by day requires you to value God's Word more than your own comfort.

The Bible says, "The integrity of the upright guides them, but the unfaithful are destroyed by their duplicity" (Prov. 11:3 NIV). It also says, "Whoever can be trusted with very little can also be trusted with much, and whoever is dishonest with very little will also be dishonest with much" (Luke 16:10 NIV).

Choosing integrity is rarely about big things. Rather, it's about deceptions we wouldn't consider big—telling a lie, cheating on a test, something we concealed, an attitude we had, or something we said or thought or did. God may be our only witness, but the stakes are even higher and the pressure stronger when others are watching. Either way, it comes down to how much we value His opinion. Enough to do the right thing? Or do we ignore it and tell ourselves God will forgive us anyway? Integrity is choosing obedience to God's ways, no matter our audience and no matter the cost, simply because it pleases God.

4. Reaching Out

Can I be completely honest? One of the hardest, most uncomfortable things for me is reaching out to others. I've always been the shy, quiet introvert who would rather stay home and read a book than go out and talk to people. I've had to grow out of this and learn how to reach out to others with God's love because no one changed the world or led others to Christ by staying inside the four walls of their comfort zones.

I can't tell you how many times I've said no when God has asked me to (literally) step out of my comfort zone. A nudge in my heart whispered, *Go pray with that person. Share the gospel with that person . . . they need hope. Reach out and tell them you care. Tell them I love them. Invite them to church.* My heart would start pounding, my palms would sweat, my knees would shake. That's when I would begin talking myself out of it. Even though God's message was clear, my fear was clearer. I didn't want to look strange or feel awkward. What if I heard wrong? What if they laughed at me and called me crazy? Over and over, I've listened to these lies and said no. So I missed out. This is still a struggle for me because I want to be obedient. I don't want to miss out anymore or stay inside where it's safe.

Jesus commands us to be a city on a hill. He tells us to go out and salt the earth with His love (see Matt. 5:13–16). But many of us are hiding our light under a basket. What might happen if we took the risk? No revival ever started with a group of Christians who were too scared to reach out.

Even if our knees are shaking, let's be bold enough to step across the line, take a chance, and be the light and love of Jesus to a world that desperately needs both.

Three Ways to Overcome the Uncomfortable

Now that we've covered some of the uncomfortable things we might encounter in this Christian life, let's break down three things we can do to help us be brave when we're faced with those situations.

1. Pray

I know it sounds cliché, but prayer really is our best weapon against fear. God understands our fears, and (get this!) He wants us to come to Him with them. I believe God can use our fears to draw us closer to Himself. When you're uncomfortable and afraid, talk to Him about those fears and ask for His peace to flood your soul and for the courage to do what He's set before you.

2. Read and Quote Scripture

The Bible is full of commands not to fear. Here's a sampling:

Fear not, for I am with you; be not dismayed, for I am your God. I will strengthen you, yes I will help you, I will uphold you with My righteous right hand. (Isa. 41:10)

Be anxious for nothing, but in everything by prayer and supplication, with thanksgiving, let your requests be made known to God; and the peace of God which surpasses all understanding will guard your hearts and minds through Christ Jesus. (Phil. 4:6–7)

Have I not commanded you? Be strong and of good courage; do not be afraid . . . for the LORD your God is with you wherever you go. (Josh. 1:9)

For God has not given us a spirit of fear, but of power and of love and of a sound mind. (2 Tim. 1:7)

The message is clear: don't fear. Be strong.

Notice God doesn't say, "Just get over your fear! Why are you so weak?" He knows our weaknesses but promises to override them with His strength. What we're called to do is lean into that strength and stand upon His promises, even when—*especially when*—we're feeling fearful and uncomfortable.

3. Step Out in Faith

Eventually it comes down to taking the first step in faith. If we wait until all our fears are gone, we'll be waiting a long time. God meets us with His peace when we fearfully take the first step.

Stepping outside our comfort zone is where radical obedience happens. Are we daring enough to declare that we'll follow God wherever He asks us to go—even if we don't know where that might be? He doesn't reveal the destination before we make the commitment. He just says, "Trust Me."

If He calls you to stand alone, you stand. If He calls you to tell the truth, you open your mouth. If He asks you to get over your fear and call a friend to pray for them, you pick up the phone. If He calls you to be a missionary overseas, you buy a plane ticket. If He asks you to fight against abortion, you do. If He nudges you to sit with the new kid at school, you grab the chair next to them.

You may not know the why or the how but God does, and all He asks is that you're willing to take the next step, no matter how hard it may be or what it may cost. We've been scratching the surface on stepping outside our comfort zones, but it's time to go deeper.

Faith Like the Martyrs

Jesus said, "Whoever desires to come after Me, let him deny himself, and take up his cross, and follow Me. For whoever desires to save his life will lose it, but whoever loses his life for My sake and the gospel's will save it" (Mark 8:34–35).

When He said this, Jesus was fully aware of the death He would die on the cross, but those He spoke to were not. By advising those around Him to take up their cross, He was challenging them to pick up their own form of execution and follow Him to the hill where He would give His life. He was asking them to follow Him in *all* ways, no matter what, even to the point of dying the same death *for Him* that He would die *for them*.

I don't know if any of us will ever have to make such a radical decision and literally lay down our lives for the sake of Christ. But I do know, without any doubt, that we're called to live for Him. And living for Him fully means denying ourselves. It means sacrificing our wants—our comforts—and nailing them to the cross.

In order to move past our comfort zones, we first have to lay them down, crucify them and, in exchange, pick up a cross of self-sacrifice.

One evening recently, I was reading stories of people that had been martyred for Christ. Their strength and faith in the middle of horrendous, unthinkable torture was at once inspiring and disturbing. I couldn't wrap my mind around their courageous behavior. Fear filled my heart as I imagined what they went through, and I wondered, *Would I have the same strength in their situation?*

I'd like to wholeheartedly say yes. But all I can do is pray, *Jesus, give me Your strength.*

Earlier that day, I prayed, *God, set my heart on fire with passion for You.* And I realized that's where it all starts. With a desire to know God and love Him, followed by a commitment to follow Him beyond our comfort zones, however shaky that commitment may be. And as we follow, our passion will grow.

I realize that in comparison to those martyrs, my sacrifices are woefully small. The examples in this chapter are, admittedly, small steps outside our comfort zones. But being faithful with the small sacrifices is important too. We'll never be willing to give up our lives for Christ if we're not willing to give up our comfort—even if it seems a small sacrifice in the big picture.

If being uncomfortable is what it takes, so be it.

If following God into the unknown is what's required, I'll follow with the words, "Lord, help me."

If smashing my comfort zones is what needs to happen to draw me closer to my Savior, let 'em fall.

I'm all-in.

— Going Deeper —

1. What's the hardest thing you've done outside your comfort zone? What did you learn from it?

2. Which uncomfortable things do you find the hardest? Living a countercultural life, standing apart, choosing integrity, or reaching out? Why?

3. Is there something in your life that you personally struggle with that gives you anxiety? Why is it hard for you to overcome? What's a practical way you can start to move beyond it today?

4. What are your favorite Scripture verses on fear? Pick two and memorize them before the end of the week.

5. Do you think you would have the strength to follow Christ to the point of dying for Him? Why or why not? Take a few minutes right now and pray for courage and strength to follow Christ wherever He would lead you this week. Look for opportunities to go beyond your comfort zone and be faithful to follow through.

6

everything means *everything*

giving your all

Jim Elliot could have done anything he wanted.

Well-liked and respected among his fellow college students, he was handsome and talented, with a wide grin, a sharp sense of humor, and unpretentious charm. As well as being one of the best wrestlers on campus, he had a gift for acting and public speaking. His unconventional opinions and radical convictions—and boldness in sharing them—coupled with his incredible oratory skills, made him particularly unforgettable. You couldn't know Jim Elliot and not recognize that there was something distinctly different about this college student from Oregon.

Yet none of that mattered to Jim. He had one goal in life. One purpose.

To live for Christ and bring Him glory.

Jim's dream was to go to Ecuador and share the gospel. Again, his purpose was resolute and his goal simple: to glorify God and share Jesus Christ.

And he was willing to give anything to see that goal accomplished. "God, I pray Thee," Jim wrote in his journal in 1948. "Light these idle sticks of my life and may I burn for Thee. Consume my life, my God, for it is Thine. I seek not a long life, but a full one, like you, Lord Jesus."[1]

After planning, dreaming, and experiencing delay upon delay, Jim finally sailed for Ecuador on February 4, 1952. He was twenty-four years old. After spending five and a half months in Quito, the capital of Ecuador, learning the language, and staying with local missionaries, he headed to the mission station at Shandia, a small village in the middle of the rain forest. But Jim had one more audacious desire—to go where the gospel had never been proclaimed, to a people never before reached. To the Huaorani tribe, also known as the Auca Indians, an infamously violent people group, deep in the heart of the Ecuadorian jungle. Jim once said, "The will of God is always a bigger thing than we bargain for."[2] In the case of attempting to reach the Huaorani people with the love of Christ, that couldn't have been more true.

After years of preparing, learning as much of the Huaorani language as possible, and attempting to befriend the tribe by dropping gifts by airplane, it was time to embark on Operation Auca. Jim and four other young men—Nate Saint, Ed McCully, Pete Fleming, and Roger Youderian—decided it was time to meet face-to-face with the Huaorani people. They knew the risks. No outsider was welcome in Huaorani territory. But their love for the gospel was too great to give up an opportunity to share it. Jim told his wife, Elisabeth, before leaving, "If God wants it that way . . . I am ready to die for the salvation of the Aucas."[3]

On Monday, January 2, 1956, the five men departed, unsure of what they would encounter, but with a fire for God in their hearts. By Friday, "the thrill of Jim's lifetime was given. He took an Auca by the hand."[4] Elisabeth later wrote, recounting the experience, "Two days later, on Sunday, January 8, 1956, the men for whom Jim Elliot had prayed for six years killed him and his four companions."[5]

Five young men. One gospel. One passion.

And devastating loss.

Elisabeth wrote in Jim's biography,

Jim's aim was to know God. His course, obedience—the only course that could lead to the fulfillment of that aim. His end was what some would call an extraordinary death, although in facing death he had quietly pointed out that many have died because of obedience to God . . . Is the distinction between living for Christ and dying for Him, after all, so great? Is not the second the logical conclusion of the first? Furthermore, to live for God is to die, "daily," as the apostle Paul put it. It is to lose everything that we may gain Christ. It is in thus laying down our lives that we find them.[6]

And for Jim, Nate, Ed, Pete, and Roger, there was no greater privilege than to lay down their lives for something far greater. After all, it was Jim who famously wrote, "He is no fool who gives that which he cannot keep to gain what he cannot lose."[7]

Indeed, they gave all.

But maybe, despite their sacrifice, they gained more.

Do You Love Enough to Give *Everything*?

Jim Elliot is one of my heroes. Everything about his life challenges and inspires me. The way he died, yes, but even more the way he lived. Committed. Surrendered. Sold out.

He gave up his time to serve God. He gave up his resources and energy to share the gospel. For five long and hard years, Jim even postponed marrying his love, Elisabeth, because he felt God calling him to live as a single missionary. He truly had one goal: to obey God and share the love of Christ. Anything hindering that goal, he was willing to sacrifice.

Reading through his journals and prayers, I wonder, *Would I be willing to give up so much? Do I love Jesus like that? Do I love Him enough to give* everything?

I pray I do. But I know I fail.

Like we talked about in the last chapter, Jesus commanded radical obedience in Mark 8:34–37, when He said,

> Whoever desires to come after Me, let him deny himself, and take up his cross, and follow Me. For whoever desires to save his life will lose it, but whoever loses his life for my sake and the gospel's will save it. For what will it profit a man if he gains the whole world and loses his own soul? Or what will a man give in exchange for his soul?

This shows me that there's no such thing as a complacent follower of Christ. You're either following Him or you aren't. You're either living for yourself or living for God. There are no "sort of" followers of Christ. There is no in-between.

Not every follower of Jesus is called to physically die for Him. But we are all called to die to ourselves—to our sin and old way of living. Paul wrote, "I have been crucified with Christ; it is no longer I who live, but Christ lives in me" (Gal. 2:20).

We often settle for going halfway with God. I know I have more times than I care to remember. We think, *Okay, God, you can have this part of my life, and that area, but don't you dare mess with these other things. Don't ask me to change this or give up that.* We hold on to sinful patterns and old habits. We're stubborn and fiercely rebellious.

I recently read an article that transformed my perspective on surrender. In it, the author wrote, "We look at Jesus and say, 'Lord, there's nothing I won't do for You. I will die for You!' But I think Jesus is responding by pointing to places in our lives and saying, 'Yes, you are willing to die for me . . . but are you willing to let this thing die *in* you?' . . . At the same instant that we are shouting, 'God, I want more of You!' He is looking back and saying, 'No, *I* want more of *you!*'"[8]

Take a minute and think about it. Can you think of any areas in your life you've been afraid to give to God? Afraid of what He'll do or how He'll ask you to change? Afraid if you allow Him to be Lord of everything, maybe He'll take away something you love?

You're not alone. I'm often afraid of what He'll ask me to give up.

My dreams? My writing? My hopes for a husband and family of my own?

I'm afraid what He'll ask me to do.

Move away? Become a missionary? Give up my life?

I've been terrified of opening my hands wide and relinquishing my fears and dreams. I've thought deep in my heart, *If I surrender this, He'll take it from me. I need to hold on tightly.*

But you see, neither of those things is true. We can't hold on, no matter how tightly we grip. God doesn't ask us to surrender to be unkind or exert His power. If He asks us to give something up, He does so with love. He knows it's hindering us from a closer relationship with Himself, is a sin in our lives, or is keeping us from something better. God won't take our surrender and throw it back in our faces.

Surrender and sacrifice are good, because God is good.

An Acceptable Sacrifice

How often do we approach the topics of sacrifice and surrender with a "how much (effort, time, devotion, etc.) do I *need* to give" mind-set, instead of a "how much do I *get* to give" mind-set?

Turn to the beginning of Genesis and you'll find an example of sacrifice so radical, so pure, so entirely devoted, it's hard to wrap your mind around.

For decades, Abraham prayed for a son. When God finally blessed him with one, Abraham couldn't believe God's next request: "Take now your son, your only son Isaac, whom you love, and go to the land of Moriah and offer him there as a burnt offering" (Gen. 22:2).

Before you get caught up in a mental argument about human sacrifice, notice one thing—God asked for the most important thing in Abraham's life. Something God had miraculously given to him—his only son. Isaac represented everything Abraham loved and held dear, his only hope for the future. And God was asking him to give him up?

Most would shake their head and say, "Absolutely not!" But that's not what we see Abraham do. Instead Abraham "rose early in the morning and saddled his donkey, and took . . . Isaac his son; and he split the wood for the burnt offering, and arose and went to the place of which God had told him" (Gen. 22:3).

Hold on. He was actually going to go through with it? I can't even imagine the pain in Abraham's heart. I can almost hear him pleading with God, "Please, not my son. Please, anything else. My life. Take my life. Just spare my son. Make another way. Why? Why are You testing me? Why ask this of me? And yet, I will obey You. I will follow You."

They made their way to the mountain. But Isaac was confused. "Father, where is the lamb for the burnt offering?"

Abraham's heart broke. He paused. "My son, God will provide."

They went farther, until they reached the spot. They built the altar, and Isaac was placed upon it as God commanded. The tension built, thick and suffocating. Until, at the last minute, God sent an angel—and a ram. "Abraham! Don't do anything to him. I now know that you fear God, since you have not withheld your son, your only son, from Me" (see Gen. 22:11–13, my paraphrase).

Isaac was spared. God provided. And Abraham showed that he was willing to give God everything—even what he loved most.

You may now be wondering, *What do Isaac and Abraham and disturbing human sacrifices have to do with me?*

It's true we no longer offer sacrifices to God like they did in the Old Testament. (God even forbids human sacrifice—see

Deut. 18:10). But these sacrifices were more than physical acts. They represented deeper sacrifices. Deeper testing and truths. Things that we, too, are called to surrender and give to God— our best, our will, our loves, our lives.

What do you value most? What is your "Isaac"? If God asked, would you be willing to give it up? If He called, would you follow?

Is it a relationship? Or a cherished dream, but God is saying, "That's not My best for you." Is it discontentment over where you are, because it's not where you want to be? Is it a bad habit you know isn't right but keep falling back to anyway? Is your social media usage distracting you from God? Or maybe what you choose to entertain yourself with?

What do you think you can't live without? A person? Hobby? Comfort zone?

What do you think would be too radical to do? Give up time to serve God? Read your Bible every day? Stop watching TV so you have time to pray? Move across the country—or even the world—to be a missionary? Give up a year of college to do mission work?

What do you think would be unfathomable and unthinkable to give up? What piece of your life are you holding back for yourself? What part of everything is excluded?

What if God asked you to give it up?

I don't know if He will, but I do know He asks for our all, no matter what that may include. The point is not to give something up for the mere sake of denying ourselves. Rather, it's evaluating our lives for hidden idols or deep-seated fears that we place above God. Anything—even good things—can become idols or places of compromise. Sometimes these are tangible—an unhealthy relationship, a possession we cling to, a lifestyle we know isn't pure. Other times they are intangible—a fear crippling our lives, an insecurity weighing us down, or a lie we believe. It's not always big areas He seeks. It's the small things we hold on to the tightest. But often these small, inconsequential areas keep us from fully living for God.

For me, some of these have been very small sacrifices but sacrifices nonetheless.

I've given up casual dating, because I want to serve God while I'm single, and I believe relationships shouldn't be taken lightly. I've had to surrender my fear of perpetual singleness and sometimes my hopes and dreams of a particular young man. I've told Him, *God, You choose!* when my heart desperately wanted to choose for myself. I've spent Friday nights by myself, answered everyone's well-meaning questions (yet again) with, "No, I'm not in a relationship," watched girls around me with boyfriends, and seen countless Facebook status updates. It seems like a small sacrifice, but it's been a sacrifice—often painful—even so. But I choose it because I want to honor my future husband and focus on God until He brings the right person into my life.

I've given up some friends, because they were walking a path I didn't want to follow. I've been snubbed and ignored and stood by myself while a group of girls I knew pretended I wasn't there. In order to fit in with them, I would've had to compromise and say and do things that go against how I feel God wants me to act. But God means more to me than the price of standing alone at a party or gathering.

There are two sides to genuine sacrifice: internal surrender and external actions. Each of these things God called me to sacrifice started in my heart with Him bringing them to light through time spent in Scripture and prayer. Then I had real and practical choices to make.

Relinquishing control begins as a heart attitude and mindset of submission, but that's not where it ends. Willingness to surrender is the foundation for our actions of surrender. Sacrifice without action isn't sacrifice at all. For example, it would be contradictory to surrender media and entertainment use, and then watch a movie that isn't honoring to God the next night. In the same way, if I'd told God I was surrendering my love life to Him, then went on a date with a guy who wasn't a Christian, my actions wouldn't line up with my heart attitude. A mind-set of surrender and an outward show of control cannot coexist.

I cannot give you a personal road map for surrender, but I know God can. Honestly ask Him, *What is keeping me from You? What do I need to sacrifice to draw closer to You?* Hand over control, give Him the keys to your life, and then listen for His call to action. When He calls, follow through. Don't wait for the feelings of surrender to take the next step on your action plan. Surrender and sacrifice aren't feelings—they're daily choices in obedience to God. Like Abraham, true surrender and sacrifice are embodied in our actions, even if those actions are hard and painful. As we commit ourselves to Him, we commit that we'll do what He asks, go where He leads, and when the time comes for action, we'll step out in trust and faith.

Count the Cost

In Luke 14, Jesus told two parables—one about a builder, the other about a king. In the first parable, the builder was working on a tower, but he didn't figure out how much it would cost and was only able to lay the foundation. The second parable tells the story of a king who was going to war, but he didn't count on the size of his rival's army and, in order to spare his vastly outnumbered men, had to ask for conditions of peace before the battle even began. What builder doesn't calculate the cost of the tower he intends to construct before he begins? Likewise, what king goes to war without considering the might of his enemy? The message in both examples?

Count the cost.

Count the price that needs to be paid before you start, or you risk not being able to finish. Following Jesus comes with a cost. There's always a price to be paid. Sometimes the cost is great—it could be your life. Other times smaller, but no less important, things must be offered. Sound radical? Listen to Jesus's own words: "So likewise, whoever of you does not forsake all that he has cannot be My disciple" (Luke 14:33). Let me ask again. What is He calling you to surrender?

To be honest, I don't have this figured out. I don't say these things as if they're easy. They're not. I struggle daily.

But I'm so thankful that Jesus is continually sanctifying me, convicting me, offering grace upon grace. I pray I'm more surrendered today than I was yesterday. And hopefully tomorrow I'll be more surrendered than I am today. But even more, I pray He sees in me, despite my flaws and failings, a heart that says, "Yes, Lord. I surrender."

We can give everything, because God *is* everything.

It's time to count the cost.

Don't settle for going halfway.

— Going Deeper —

1. What stood out to you in Jim Elliot's story?
2. What stood out to you in the story of Abraham and Isaac (e.g., Abraham's heart attitude, level of obedience)?
3. Read Philippians 3:7–8. What do you think it means that even though we're giving something (a thing, attitude, mind-set, lifestyle), in reality we're gaining something (God)? Is this true? Why do you think it would be worth it?
4. What do you think God is asking you to surrender? How can you obey Him and follow through?
5. Are you willing to give your all? Why or why not? How are you struggling with this? Talk to God and ask for His strength.

PART THREE

the challenge

7

raising the battle cry

you're in the fight of your life

God, what's wrong with me? I thought, as I desperately tried to get my mind back on track.

I turned from where I'd been reading in Mark, and like a switch had been flipped, distractions bombarded my heart. Everything I'd just been contemplating flew out the window and was replaced with a sense of stress. My mind filled with thoughts about my enormous to-do list for the day, how behind I was on everything, how much time I'd been wasting lately, even scenes from the movie I'd watched with my family the night before. Frustrated, I forced myself to concentrate on the passage in front of me, but my thoughts were already spinning a million miles an hour, all concentration crushed.

Then it dawned on me. This was like the parable of the farmer sowing seeds that I'd just read. More than a case of simply being distracted, this was an outright attack to steer me off the path of learning God's truth. Seeds had been sown in my heart and the devil wasn't happy about it, so he was trying to devour those seeds before they took root (see Mark 4:4).

I realized this important truth: the enemy will do anything to distract us from drawing closer to Christ.

This wasn't an unusual occurrence. It's actually more familiar than I'd like to admit. But Satan is an expert at using the small and commonplace to distract us from God. You might have experienced similar times in your life. Maybe even as you've been reading this book. You're convicted in your relationship with Christ, seeds are sown, and love begins to bloom. You start taking action, and then—*bam*! Your mind is overrun with distractions, temptations, reasons why it doesn't matter, why drawing close to God is too much work. Compromise starts creeping in. Lies infiltrate your heart. You get discouraged, worn down, and weary. *Shouldn't this be coming easier?* you wonder. So you give up. Stop trying. And those seeds are devoured by the enemy of our souls.

We have a very real opponent. Satan is God's enemy and as God's children, he's also our enemy, along with the demons that follow him. They're out to defeat us, especially when we're young. And especially when we start to get serious about our relationship with God.

You are a target.

I don't mean to scare you, but I'm warning you so you're equipped and understand there's a battle before us. The second you give your life to Christ, you cross over a line. You step from Satan's camp to God's camp. You're branded with the name "Christian" and everyone possessing that name is a target. Because our enemy is tenacious. He doesn't leave followers of Christ alone. He goes after them, trying to lure them closer and closer to the line, attempting to fill their lives with misery, temptation, and pain. There are so many lukewarm Christians and halfhearted followers, because the seeds sown in their hearts are getting choked out (Mark 4:7), dried up (Mark 4:6), or stolen (Mark 4:4).

One of my favorite books, *The Screwtape Letters* by C. S. Lewis, powerfully illustrates this. The book records the correspondence between Screwtape, a senior demon, to his nephew Wormwood, about the young man Wormwood is in charge of drawing away from God (The Enemy, as they call Him) and toward Satan (Our Father Below). It's an eye-opening read of how Satan works to distract, tempt, and lead us away from Christ.

For example, Screwtape advises Wormwood not to win the young man with arguments but to simply confuse him enough that he won't know what he believes—except that it's not in God. He shares a time when one of his "patients," a sound atheist, began to doubt what he believed.

> One day, as he sat reading, I saw a train of thought in his mind beginning to go the wrong way. The Enemy, of course, was at his elbow in a moment. Before I knew where I was I saw my twenty years' work beginning to totter. If I had lost my head and begun to attempt a defence by argument I should have been undone. But I was not such a fool. I struck instantly at the part of the man which I had best under my control and suggested that it was just about time he had some lunch. . . . He is now safe in Our Father's house.[1]

While *The Screwtape Letters* is fictional, the truths it shares are not. We have a real enemy, and it's his mission to defeat followers of God. His weapons range from distractions and peer pressure, to temptations and lies, to things steeped in the occult and demonic forces, to simply suggesting lunch (to name a few). He strikes where we're weak, and every weapon he wields is a lie. We have to be wise, discerning, and aware of this battle that's raging. If we're not aware, we won't be able to fight against it.

Dear Teen, This is Your Battle Plan

Every warrior needs a battle plan. Ours is found in Scripture. God has revealed to us several powerful and effective ways to resist the attacks of the enemy through the power of Christ. Let's go over four practical battle strategies that glorify God and cause Satan to flee.

1. Understand Your Enemy

I don't know what your background is with these concepts. Some churches never speak about Satan, demons, or hell. They try to pretend they don't exist because they're uncomfortable and scary topics. This may be the first time you're hearing how Satan works. On the other hand, some churches and denominations go overboard and speak about the devil constantly. I think there needs to be a balance. It's a dark world, so we need to understand Satan. It's important to realize that darkness and demons are real, but ultimately, we need to make sure our focus is on Christ.

If this is a new and slightly disturbing topic for you, please understand that it doesn't have to be. Yes, Satan is real and his methods can be powerful. They've overtaken much of our world. But God is more powerful than all the powers of the devil, so no matter how hard he tries, Satan cannot win. I know who wins the battle because I've read the end of the story (Rev. 20–22). God is the victor; Satan is crushed.

It's because we already know the end of the story that Satan tries to defeat us. He knows he can't win, but he'll attempt to sabotage God's plans as much as possible. He knows our potential, the power of God's call on our lives, and it's his goal to ruin our future and the impact we'll have.

Satan is the father of lies (John 8:44), so lies are one of his strongest weapons. He seeks to confuse us and degrade God's truth. Just think of how he deceived Eve in the garden of Eden. He questioned God's truth, "Has God indeed said, 'You shall not eat of every tree of the garden'?" (Gen. 3:1). Then he further reduced God's words and spoke lies and half-truths by telling her, "You will not surely die" (Gen. 3:4).

The thing about Satan's tactics is that he doesn't have any new ones. He may not be trying to get us to eat a piece of fruit anymore, but he uses the same patterns again and again. Questioning God. Trying to confuse us and get us to doubt. Whispering lies. Degrading truth. Muddying the waters. He mixes just a little bit of evil into good, increases the dose bit by bit, until goodness is lost in evil and light is doused by darkness. By understanding these tactics, we won't be as likely to fall for them.

2. Focus on Christ

I once heard the phrase, "Don't be a thermometer. Be a thermostat." A thermometer measures the temperature and conditions of its location. It's able to sense the climate, but it doesn't do anything to change the atmosphere. A thermostat, on the other hand, reads the conditions, and puts into action the necessary forces to adjust the temperature.

There are too many Christians who live like thermometers. They sense evil in the world and might even sense the devil attacking them, but instead of going on the offensive, they merely "read the atmosphere." They understand Satan, but they're not taking the weapons God has given them, fighting back, and inviting Christ to come in and invade the spiritual atmosphere.

As we focus on Christ, we're taking hold of the weapons He has provided. Praise is one of the most beautiful ways to fix our eyes on God, and it's also one of the most powerful weapons against Satan! The enemy can't withstand the pure praises of God's people. When we praise God despite our circumstances, chains are broken, strongholds crushed, walls destroyed, and armies defeated. Think of Paul and Silas praising God in prison (Acts 16:25–26). Jehoshaphat leading his army praising into battle (2 Chron. 20:15–24). The Israelites praising the walls of Jericho down in obedience to God (Josh. 6).

Prayer is another powerful way to focus on Christ. Author Samuel Chadwick said, "Satan dreads nothing but prayer. His one concern is to keep the saints from praying. He fears nothing from prayerless studies, prayerless work, prayerless religion. He laughs at our toil, he mocks our wisdom, but he trembles when we pray."[2] Prayer is more powerful than we realize. When we pray, we're entering the throne room of God while also stepping onto the battlefield. Over and over in Scripture we see proof of answered prayer. When Daniel set his heart to pray and fast for three weeks, God sent an angel to him, and Daniel's prayers covered the exact amount of time the angel struggled against the evil forces delaying him (Dan. 10:1–14). Elijah prayed fervently seven times for God to end the drought plaguing Israel, and on the seventh time, God sent rain (1 Kings 18:41–45). And James told us, "The effective, fervent prayer of a righteous man avails much" (James 5:16).

To be a strong warrior in the kingdom of God, we first have to be submerged in the presence of God. Focusing on Christ gives us a different perspective. It's true that Satan's oppression can sometimes feel suffocating and overpowering, but the good news is that, as Christ followers, we don't have to succumb to it. As we focus on God, we'll suddenly understand that the "battle is not [ours], but God's" (2 Chron. 20:15).

3. Saturate Your Heart with Truth

Let's flash back two thousand years. It had been forty days— forty nights. No food. No companionship. All around was nothing but wilderness. As God made into flesh, Jesus endured this pressure, but as a man, He was weakening.

The devil entered with taunts and tricks, his words slick. He was fully aware of Christ's humanity, and he planned to use it to defame His deity. Can you hear the enemy's words? "If You are the Son of God, command that these stones become bread" (Matt. 4:3).

Zoom out to where Jesus was. How did He fight against this attack? In two words: with truth. "It is written, 'Man shall not live by bread alone, but by every word that proceeds from the mouth of God'" (Matt. 4:4).

Three times the devil attacked. Three times Jesus counterattacked with Scripture and three small words: it is written.

Scripture is powerful and truth-packed. The devil attacks with lies. Lies about our identity, our worth, our purpose. Lies about our hearts, sexuality, futures, needs, and desires. Lies about theology, the purpose of being a Christian, and even God's love for us. He whispers deceptions, taking a truth and twisting and distorting it until it's no longer true but shadowed in enough truth that we'll believe it. He even spoke Jesus's own words back to Him and quoted Scripture to the Son of God (see Matt. 4:6).

But Jesus wasn't buying these tricks. He was saturated in God's truth, and even the devil's shadowy half-truths couldn't fool Him.

That's what we need to be if we're going to have a chance at discerning truth from lies—saturated in God's Word. I often pray, *God, lead me to a knowledge of the truth* (see 2 Tim. 3:7). But as I pray, I know I must also search the Word, asking for eyes of understanding and a spirit of wisdom (see Eph. 1:17–18).

Hebrews 4:12 says, "For the word of God is living and powerful, and sharper than any two-edged sword, piercing even to the division of soul and spirit, and of joints and marrow, and is a discerner of the thoughts and intents of the heart." To discern truth, we must stand upon God's Word and evaluate everything through its pages. But to do so, we need to be familiar with it. Just like someone skilled in fencing and swordsmanship wouldn't go against an opponent with an unfamiliar weapon, we can't fall back on God's Word only when we need it or we'll be clumsy and unfamiliar with our spiritual sword.

While the devil is skilled in lies, God is skilled in truth. When Satan tries to feed you lies, pull out your Bible and replace those lies with the truth God has given you. We can hold in our hands, and speak with our mouths, words of unprecedented, immeasurable power.

4. Submit to God

James 4:7 tells us, "Therefore submit to God. Resist the devil and he will flee from you."

We often look at this verse and go straight to the "resist the devil" part. But resistance without submission is futile. In our own strength, we have no power whatsoever to resist the devil. We must first be equipped with the power of the Holy Spirit by submitting to God.

Submitting to God looks like giving up our will and surrendering to His. It looks like quieting our hearts and spending time with Him. It looks like letting Him do a makeover in our souls, bending, shaping, and molding us to look more like Him. It looks like drawing near to God, because as James tells us in the next verse, "Draw near to God and He will draw near to you. Cleanse your hands . . . purify your hearts" (4:8).

These are our most powerful methods of defeating the enemy, because they get down to the heart of what he is trying to destroy—our relationship with God. The stronger we are in Christ, the more hedged we are with the protection of His presence. Fighting against the enemy sometimes looks much less like fighting and much more like simply being still and soaking in God's presence. Surrendering to His will. Getting closer to His heart and falling more in love with Christ, praying fervently and without ceasing. That is what Satan is trying to destroy, because that is the exact thing that makes him flee.

Put On Your Armor, Teenager

I have never experienced more spiritual attack than while writing this book. I can only describe the first few months of writing as *painful.* My mind was bombarded with doubts and fear as Satan hurled lies at me.

You're not a writer! You're going to sound like an idiot.

You can't write a whole book! Why not give up and leave writing to the professionals?

You sound like a hypocrite. Why should people believe you when you're such a mess yourself?

These lies are the reason my mom found me crumpled up and sobbing on the basement floor. Why I laid awake at night, plagued with doubt and insecurity. Why I woke up filled with anxiety and cried as I told my sister I didn't think I could do it. Why I wrote in my journal one desperate day, "God, I'm scared. *I DON'T WANT TO WRITE THIS BOOK ON MY OWN!*"

But I pressed on. I didn't give up. If Satan was going to try this hard to make me doubt myself, you'd better believe I was not going to back down and let him win—no matter how hard it was to press on.

Satan *will* attack us as we follow Christ. He will attempt to hurl lies at us, slither temptations by us, make us compromise and give up. I don't always know how he works and I don't know how he might attempt to invade your life, but I do know this: he doesn't have the final word.

That belongs to God.

Ephesians 6:10 says, "Finally, my brethren, be strong in the Lord and in the power of His might."

It's time to be strong in the Lord. To put on the full armor He's given us. To pray and seek and submit and draw near. To saturate our hearts with truth and live like Jesus is the victor.

Because on the cross, Christ defeated Satan once and for all. It's through the mighty name of Jesus Christ that we have victory. "That at the name of Jesus every knee should bow, of those in heaven and of those on earth and of those under the earth, and that every tongue should confess that Jesus Christ is Lord, to the glory of God the Father" (Phil. 2:10–11).

Put on your armor, fellow warrior. It's time to raise the battle cry and declare that Jesus Christ is Lord.

So pick up your sword. Know it well and wield it skillfully. Put on the whole armor that is given you. Place truth about your waist, and strap on the breastplate of righteousness. Slip into the shoes of the gospel of peace, and take up the shield of faith which is able to thwart all the enemy's plans of attack. Place upon your head the helmet called salvation, and fall on your knees in battle (see Eph. 6:14–17).

Yes, this is a battle. But Jesus has already won the war.

— Going Deeper —

1. Is the idea of spiritual battles and attacks from Satan new to you? Do you find it scary or disturbing? Why or why not?

2. Have you ever experienced distractions like those described at the beginning of the chapter? What did you make of them and how does this chapter change your perspective?

3. Which of the four points do you find the hardest? Why do you think they're effective against the enemy?

4. What specific lies has the enemy tried to tell you? What does Scripture say in comparison? Does it assure you that God has the final word and is already victorious?

5. How do you feel the enemy has attacked you in the past? Prepare a "battle strategy" by coming up with several Scripture verses that combat it. Set aside time today to focus on God and spend time in His presence.

8

seeking hard . . . or hardly seeking?

let's spend some time with Jesus

Let's be real. We all struggle. One of the most common struggles I've heard from teens again and again is how to spend time with God. I hear things like:

- I'm frustrated. I've grown so distant from God.
- I haven't been reading my Bible, because I feel stuck. I keep pushing it aside, and now I don't know where to start.
- I don't know how to genuinely pray. I try, but it feels more like leaving a message on God's answering machine than actually spending time with Him.

These questions and frustrations always hit close to my heart, because I completely understand. We all experience times when our relationship with God feels distant. Believe me, I've been there. I've yawned my way through Leviticus and questioned what on earth the book of Numbers has to do with me. I've found myself gazing into space in the middle of my prayer time, completely forgetting what I was praying about. And I've made excuses and pushed aside my time with God.

All our excuses are simply that—excuses. When we say things like, "I can't seem to feel God when I pray," "The Bible never seems applicable to me," or "I don't have time to study the Bible and pray," it's really just our way of saying, "It isn't important to me." We think we're seeking hard and coming up empty, but in reality, we're hardly seeking.

What Spending Time with God Is (And What It's Not)

There are two major ways to spend time with God: Bible study and prayer. You might think they're separate, but they're actually closely connected. The thing they have in common is that they're both channels of communication with God.

Through the Bible we learn God's heart. Through prayer we pour out our own. In the Bible we discover His plans and promises and also His ways and commands. In prayer we ask for His help and strength and listen to His Spirit. In the Bible we learn how to praise and worship. Through prayer we offer praise and worship. Both draw us closer to the heart of God and into His presence.

I'm going to get really practical in the next two chapters, but before we talk about what these practices are, let's talk about what they're *not*.

Time with God shouldn't be a rushed five minutes before you head out the door or a sleepy ten minutes before you fall into bed. It's not grabbing your phone and reading two verses or picking up a one-minute devo book. It's not giving God a to-do list with deadlines. If that's all it was, it would be an incredibly one-sided, self-centered relationship.

And that's what the things we sometimes refer to as devotions, quiet time, or Bible study really are—the development of a *relationship*. Like all relationships, our relationship with God requires hard work and consistency to grow and thrive.

Easy and *fun* isn't how I would describe it; more like *rewarding* and *joy-filled*. You can't simply fit time with God in; you have to make it a priority. But it's also important to understand that it's a joy and not a duty. Reading Scripture and praying are not pleas to earn God's favor, because we already have it through Christ. We don't do them to beg God to be with us, because He already is. It's not a checkmark on our "good Christian to-do list" but an act of intimacy, of drawing nearer to God, learning who He is, and how to follow and obey Him. It's making the relationship our own, instead of settling for a secondhand faith.

When I take the time to quiet my spinning mind and focus on Jesus, I find a friendship unlike any other. And I know every second with Him is time well spent. I want to know Jesus, and the only way I'll get to know Him is by spending time with Him. All my excuses vanish when I take time to seek hard after God.

Let's dig in and learn about the first aspect of this relationship—prayer.

Prayer: A Two-Way Exchange

Prayer is perhaps the hardest Christian discipline to master. Anyone who's ever struggled with distractions and a wandering mind while trying to pray knows this is true. But it's also one of the most powerful, important, and joy-filled ways to connect with God. I've heard it said that being a Christian who doesn't pray is no more possible than living without breathing.[1] From my own experience, I'd have to agree.

I recently got back from a trip to Tennessee. It was hectic and busier than I expected, and I barely had time to think, let alone spend time in prayer. After I got home, it was the same way. I was in a flurry of unpacking and catching up on everything that had been neglected. I was still fitting in a few minutes every day to read the Bible, but my soul was beginning to get parched for God's presence.

I could feel the difference, going from spending time with God every day, to barely catching half a minute a day for prayer. I didn't have the same peace and joy. I was irritable and stressed. My soul started to shrivel from lack of time with God. I was spiritually starving.

Prayer Is a Lifestyle

The past several years I've developed the habit of spending time in prayer every morning. The amount of time has varied over the years, from spending more than an hour in prayer to barely scraping together ten minutes. I've had my fair share of missed days as well.

I wouldn't trade these sacred moments for anything. But a year after I started, I began to notice something. After I finished up in the morning, I rarely prayed again for the remainder of the day. I put a check next to "prayer" on my mental to-do list and then forgot about it until the next morning. Without even realizing it, I was missing out on an important aspect of prayer.

First Thessalonians 5:17 says, "Pray without ceasing." I used to think this meant you had to pray all the time. And I was confused about how on earth *anyone* could possibly do that. I mean, duh, we have lives to live here. But Paul doesn't actually mean we have to spend all day on our knees praying. (Relieved?) What he's saying here is to make prayer a lifestyle. A constant mind-set and practice.

While I had a great prayer time every morning (or felt guilty for missing), I failed miserably on this "pray without ceasing" stuff. I needed both. Prayer isn't a boxed-in, once-a-day thing. It's close communion with God that occurs all day long. It's praising Him when we see His hand at work and thanking Him for the gifts He gives. It's focusing our minds on Him and bringing our requests and needs to Him, talking to Him about our day, and asking for His strength, help, and guidance. Sometimes it's a simple, desperate, and to-the-point, *God, help me!* Ceaseless prayer is like whispering to a best friend all day long and intimately drawing close to your Creator and Savior.

Ceaseless prayer is hard work. I don't know about you, but my mind isn't wired to automatically focus on God. It's not easy to reroute the channels of our minds. But we actually have so many opportunities to talk with God. What if we prayed while we're in the car? What if we prayed while we're washing the dishes or doing chores? The next time you're bored or find your mind wandering, use it as an opportunity to come before God. Don't settle for just ten minutes or even half an hour a day. Prayer isn't something we do and check off but something we *live.*

Prayer Is Consistent Communication with God

On the other hand, we desperately need focused, one-on-one time with God. Making prayer a lifestyle is only possible if we also take the time for intentional, focused prayer. Believe it or not, God longs to hear from you. That's why He created prayer as a way of communication between humans and Himself. Psalm 116:1–2 says, "I love the LORD, because He has heard my voice and my supplications. Because He has inclined His ear to me, therefore I will call upon Him as long as I live."

This system of prayer is a marvelous thing. God doesn't need our prayers, but He does want them. He desperately loves us, wants to hear from us, and "inclines His ear" when we call upon Him. Think of God leaning in to catch every word we say, because He loves the sound of our voices. As we pray, our relationship with Him grows and flourishes, multidimensional and intimate. Through sin, humanity lost deep intimacy with God, but through prayer, it's restored. There's beauty and unimaginable love to be found when we seek the face of our Savior.

Yet we still turn away. We aren't intentional. We're distracted and promise we'll do it "later." But of course, "later" never comes.

What's wrong with us?

Part of it has to do with our own guilt and sinfulness. We feel we're not worthy, and we would be right. But when Jesus died and rose again, He did so for unworthy people and gave us His worthiness in exchange. Another problem is that we don't think of prayer as a priority. We push it aside because other things are more demanding. And often we simply aren't organized and intentional about coming to God in prayer.

Six Tips for Spending Time in Prayer

Now that we've talked about why it's important, here are six tips on how to intentionally schedule time with God. While these are practical points, please don't interpret them as a legalistic, guilt-ridden ritual. We have to be practical and intentional, but more than anything, let's be motivated by love and a desire to get to know God. After all, prayer is simply talking and spending time with Him.

1. Give Him the Best Part of Your Day

Don't give God your leftover time. After all, who actually has any of that? Give Him the best.

First thing in the morning, before you check your phone,

before you start school or go to work, put God first. This requires intentionality and sometimes sacrifices, but it's so worth it.

2. Schedule It

I'm serious. If necessary, put a reminder on your phone or write it on your calendar. And keep the appointment. You wouldn't miss an appointment with a friend just because you were busy or something else came up, would you? Treat your time with God with the same respect. Diligently guard it and don't let anything get in the way.

3. Eliminate Distractions

This is easier said than done, but you can be intentional about clearing your mind of unnecessary distractions. Turn off your phone when you go to pray. That way you won't hear any notifications, and you won't be tempted to check them. Tell your family not to bother you when you're praying, and be sure you actually spend the time praying. Don't take advantage of the time alone to do something else! If necessary, leave the house. Go for a walk. Sit outside. Take a short drive and pray in a parking lot or by the side of the road. Do whatever you have to do to get alone with God. He's not picky about where you are or your physical posture. He just asks that you show up.

4. Write Prayers and Prayer Requests

I love keeping a prayer journal. I don't write in it every day, but I love looking back at past entries to see what God has done and how I've grown closer to Him. Sometimes I'm still waiting for an answer or sometimes the answer was no, but either way, it's a testimony of His faithfulness.

Find a journal or notebook and write down your prayers and prayer requests. Having them in front of you can help provide focus and direction as you pray and keep your mind on what you're praying for.

5. Know What You're Going to Pray For and When

I recently heard about a young man who leaves for his college classes a few minutes early every morning to spend the extra time in his car praying for his classmates and teachers. His plan is three-fold: One, to make sure he prays for his school every day. Two, so he can head into class with a missions-focused mind-set by praying directly beforehand. And three, to set aside undivided time to cover this specific area in prayer, instead of trying to fit it into his usual prayer time. His passion and intentionality inspired me.

I used to struggle (and often still do) with feeling like there were too many prayer requests and not enough time. As a result, I often prayed halfheartedly, rushing through my list to get to the item at the bottom so I could move on with my life—total transparency here! It left me feeling stressed instead of connected to God.

The truth is that there are so many different things that need prayer. As you spend more time with God, you'll become increasingly aware of them.

My problem was that I wasn't organized. I didn't know what to pray for. I said I would pray for someone, and then I'd forget. Or I wanted to pray for specific causes, and then I would run out of time. Organization has helped with this tremendously. There are things I pray for daily—like my family and friends. Then there are other things I pray for consistently, but instead of trying to cram all the needs of the world into one day, I schedule days and times to pray for certain subjects. By focusing on what I'm praying for and being organized, I'm better able to fervently intercede on that specific topic.

Don't forget that there's great power in prayer. And yes, that even includes *your* prayers. The power isn't found in the person praying, or the words said, but the One we pray to. So don't worry about the words or if you're doing it "correctly" or not. Just show up and intentionally come before God. Like the disciples in Luke 11:1, we can ask Jesus to teach us to pray, and He will.

6. Put in the Hard Work

We often approach prayer in a sloppy and casual way. Does this sound familiar? *Um . . . God . . . um . . . thank you . . . uh . . . help me with this test . . . uh (what am I praying for again?) . . . um . . . be with so-and-so . . . um . . . thank you, Amen.*

Don't tell me you haven't prayed something similar at least once. I sure have. Imagine if you were having a conversation and that's all the effort the other person was giving. Frustrating, right? I wouldn't want to talk to that person ever again.

Prayer is an intentional discipline. Yes, it's joy-filled and love-motivated, but we have to think about what we're praying for and put effort into it. Satan wants you to be distracted. He doesn't want you to intentionally put in the hard work of fervently crying out to God. That's why we're bombarded with so many distractions when we start to pray. My heart is often divided and unfocused when I begin my prayer time, and it feels like everything is working against me. My to-do list is calling. The clock tells me I'm already behind schedule. I'm still too sleepy. Can you relate?

What I've learned is that whenever I feel this way, I can be sure I'm in the middle of a thick battle. That means I need to get down on my knees, focus my heart, and get serious about the hard work of praying. If you feel like this, take a few minutes to focus on God by listening to worship music or reading Scripture out loud. I love to pray through Scripture as well. Setting aside a few minutes to focus your heart can help prepare you to enter the throne room of His presence.

Don't Give Up

One thing I don't want you to do after reading this chapter is think, *Okay, this sounds cool. I'll try it.* I don't want you to start strong and then slowly get out of the habit after a week or two. Why do I think you might do that? Because I've done it.

It's easy to get excited about something, get a great start, and then allow it to slowly simmer down as the days pass. That's why I'm warning you now. Don't let that happen.

Yes, your prayer time will be the freshest and most exciting the first few days. And yes, your enthusiasm will die down. Feelings will ebb and flow. Your schedule will get crazy. You'll be tempted to give up, or at least skip a day . . . or two . . . or three and on and on.

When the fire and excitement die down—keep going. When you're tired and discouraged—keep going. When you feel like you don't have time—make time. When conflicts arise and distractions come up—be intentional. When your school or work schedule changes and you don't think you can keep it up—change your prayer schedule. *But keep going.*

And when you miss a day . . . or two . . . or a week . . . or even a month, don't let that stop you from starting again. Be tenacious and fiercely protective of your time with God. Don't let anything steal it.

Seek God hard. Rouse your soul, follow after Him, and focus your heart on Him through every day and moment. Yes, you will experience apathy and sometimes you'll think it's not worth it. Don't give in to those lies. Fall on your knees and seek God's face. If you desire to passionately love God and follow Him faithfully, you *must* pray.

— Going Deeper —

1. Have you ever not felt like spending time with God? Did you spend time with Him anyway?

2. Which point was most helpful in being intentional about prayer? Pick a time and place and take steps to develop a regular prayer time today.

3. What's the difference between a daily prayer time and a lifestyle of prayer? Is either more important and how do they complement each other?

4. What distractions do you encounter most often? How can you be intentional about eliminating them?

5. Have you ever started something and then given up a few weeks later? How can you prepare so that doesn't happen with your prayer time?

9

deeper than a one-minute devo

digging into God's word

If there's one thing I've noticed about Christians, it's that we like our Bibles. And I don't necessarily mean that we're well-versed in Scripture or that our Bibles are falling apart from too much use. Quite the opposite actually.

Think about it. There are dozens of different versions. And not only are there dozens of versions, but you can get each of those versions in a unique format. Have you ever heard of a waterproof Bible or flipped through a journaling Bible? There are even Bibles with coloring pages inside. Because of the expanding number of editions in our society, we usually end up with stacks of Bibles around our homes.

Are we actually reading any of them?

While it's okay to have a special Bible or to want one that's nice, the main point of Scripture is sometimes lost in an attempt to attractively package God's words so they are more "interesting" to us. We need to get back to what the Bible is all about.

We struggle with this though. We're busy and sometimes don't find Scripture relevant to our daily lives. But getting into God's Word is not optional for a Christ follower. The Bible is how we learn about God and how He wants us to live. It's our life manual and marching orders, our perfect standard and what we evaluate everything else through. It's not a dull ritual but a lifesaving, hope-breathing, direction-giving letter that God has written to us. We can't love God and not read His words or claim to follow Him and ignore His teaching.

Without God's Word, we wouldn't know how to act or how to bring Him glory. Psalm 119:9 says, "How can a young person stay on the path of purity? By living according to your word" (NIV). Without the Word, we'd be lost without a compass. We wouldn't have the encouragement and exhortation, the stories of God's deliverance, and the examples of both good and evil. We wouldn't have the words of Christ and the story of His life.

Fortunately, we do have all these things, but instead of digging deep into these truths, we let the most dramatic, glory-filled, comforting, life-giving book collect dust on our bookshelves. Just like prayer, Bible reading isn't a check mark on our "good Christian to-do list." We don't read it to rack up points on a scorecard with God. We read it to know Him. Not just know *about* Him but *know* Him, intimately and personally. Author Francis Chan says, "God doesn't want religious duty. He doesn't want a distracted, half-hearted 'Fine, I'll read a chapter . . . now are You happy?' attitude. God wants His Word to be a delight to us, so much so that we meditate on it day and night."[1] The great news is that the more we read Scripture, the more our souls crave its words and it becomes a delight.

Four Tips for Digging into Scripture

Here are four practical ways to dig into the Word, stay consistent, and let it change your life.

1. Pray before You Read

Remember how prayer and Bible study are connected? Preparing your heart to receive God's Word through prayer is one of the most powerful ways they meet and complement each other. We're incapable of discerning the truths in Scripture on our own without the Holy Spirit's guidance. Spiritual principles need to be spiritually discerned, and prayer helps us understand the Bible. Evangelist J. C. Ryle said, "Read it with the prayer that the Holy Spirit's grace will help you understand it. It has been said, 'A man may just as soon read the Scripture without eyes, as understand the spirit of it without grace.'"[2]

Before you read, pray. Pray for wisdom to understand God's Word and for open eyes and a sensitive heart. Pray it would light your path and be a guide to your steps. Pray that you'd be challenged, encouraged, made holier and more like Christ as you read and meditate on each word. Pray that you would delight in reading the Bible and crave its words. Pray along with the psalmist, "Open my eyes, that I may see wondrous things from Your law" (119:18).

2. Read It Regularly and Read It First

Don't read the Bible occasionally. Read it every day. Scripture is food for your soul—don't starve yourself. After spending some time in prayer, the first thing I do every morning is grab my Bible. It varies how much I read. Once I read the whole Bible in a year. For several years, I read one chapter a day starting from Genesis until I reached Revelation. Sometimes I read two chapters a day, but other times, if the chapters are long, or if I feel God speaking something to my heart that I need to think about for a while, I'll stop before I finish a full chapter. Lately, I've been reading a portion from the Old Testament and then a portion from the New Testament so I'm absorbing truths from different sections of Scripture. Sometimes I find something powerful and applicable right away, while other times I have to dig a little harder.

What has been most helpful in staying consistent is that I do it *first*. Before I check my phone, before I eat breakfast, before I start writing, before the day actually begins, I'm in the Word. By doing this before anything else, I'm investing in God first, proving that He's my priority and also starting the day off with a focus on Christ.

I will admit that some days, if I sleep late (don't judge) or have to get up earlier than usual, I don't have as much time and feel rushed as a result. Some mornings I feel more distracted than others and have to work hard to focus my mind on Christ, and other mornings—let's be real—I'm just plain tired. God gives grace for those mornings, and even though I'm not at my best, I know I'm still soaking in God's words and He can use even my halfhearted efforts to speak to my heart and draw me closer to Himself.

3. Don't Just Read—Think and Study

The Bible is not a textbook you read for information or a novel you read for entertainment. It's not enough to just read it—you have to absorb it. I've been guilty of reading the chapter for the day, closing my Bible, and forgetting what I read—especially when I'm in the tough Old Testament books. It takes special discipline to slow down and actually think about the words you're reading. I've learned to pull out a verse or two and think it through. I ask myself questions like, "How does this change my perspective?" "What does this show me about God?" "Do I feel convicted?" "How can I apply this today?" Sometimes I've journaled my answers.

There's so much depth and so many truths underneath the surface of Scripture that we won't discover if we simply read the Bible like any other book. The point of studying and thinking through what we read is that it focuses our hearts on God and His ways. Merely reading might not make a dent, but meditating and contemplating what we read, and how we can apply it to our lives, changes our thoughts, hearts, and attitudes.

4. Don't Just Think—Memorize

Before you start arguing that you can't memorize, think about all the songs you have in your head. Personally, I have dozens of *I Love Lucy* episodes memorized, and it only takes listening to a song twice before I have a majority of the lyrics forever ingrained in my memory.

I never used to think I could memorize, despite the evidence I just listed to the contrary. In fact, I was so opposed to the idea that I made up excuses why I didn't have to, simply because I thought it sounded like too much work. About a year and a half ago, I decided to give it a go. I'd read a method in a book that sounded simple enough, so I thought, *Why not?*

I started big. My first goal: Philippians. Yep, the whole book. It took around five months, but I did it. It was difficult but not as difficult as I imagined. I still struggle with reviewing it and my memory isn't flawless, but I don't regret one second of the time I spent committing God's Word to memory.

You don't have to memorize whole books or even chapters to glean the benefits of memorization. You could even start with a verse a week. It doesn't matter how much you memorize but rather that you're filling your mind with God's words and letting them soak deep into your heart. Psalm 119:11 says, "Your Word I have hidden in my heart, that I might not sin against You." You never know if the time may come when you don't have access to a Bible. Wouldn't you want the Bible in your heart?

The Heart of the Matter

I don't want to make this sound like a ritual or a dry, educational process. I don't want you to think of reading your Bible simply as a discipline and not as a joy. As you dig deeper into Scripture, consistently letting its words wash over your heart, that's exactly what it becomes: a joy.

Few things have brought me as much joy as spending time with Jesus. I can't tell you how reading God's Word has flooded my soul with pure and simple delight. I've experienced moments of healing as I read, as well as moments of painful conviction. There have been times when it seemed as though God was right there, whispering in my ear, but there have also been times of dryness when I desperately needed something to revive my soul. I've cried over my Bible. I've been drawn to worship through its pages.

It's not always fun or easy. But I can tell you with 100 percent certainty it's always worth it. Ask God to give you a fiery passion for His Word. He will. And when the fire dims and flickers, ask again. If you never read another book again—or even if you don't finish this one—never give up on reading the Bible. It will lead you and sustain you. Uplift and encourage you. It's a light to guide you, a lamp to direct your steps (see Ps. 119:105). Don't let yourself get too busy. If you have to give up other things, so be it. If you have to sacrifice sleep, social media, TV, or time for yourself, that's fine. Just don't ignore God's Word.

How Far Are You Willing to Go?

Let's flash back to England in the year 1523.

Never before has the entirety of Scripture been freely published in English. The only legal Bible is in Latin and only scholars can read the original Greek and Hebrew. That is, until a twenty-nine-year-old British man named William Tyndale, a fiery scholar with a passion for God, decides that needs to change.

He's berated, criticized, and threatened for his desire to share God's Word with all people. He sees the poor and illiterate, those unable to read God's Word for themselves. He sees those tortured, imprisoned, and burned at the stake for teaching their children the Lord's Prayer and the Ten Commandments. It's illegal, you see, to read, memorize, or own Scripture in English. The consequences for doing so are extreme and deadly. Maybe the king and the church leaders are afraid of what will happen if the common people get ahold of the Word of God. Maybe they know the power it contains and fear the revival it would surely spark. However, the people's hunger and thirst for Scripture cannot—*will not*—be quenched. Not threats, not even death, will quiet their passion.

William Tyndale sees this and his heart burns with a vision for even the lowliest farmer to be able to read and teach his family the truths of the Bible. He decides to take action, knowing it could cost him everything.

After leaving England for fear of his life, he settles in Germany and works on his translation of the New Testament. Danger follows him, however, and he moves to Belgium, still translating. He's soon finished, and copies of Tyndale's New Testament are smuggled illegally into England. These little books are quickly purchased and devoured by the people, some who have never before encountered the words within. People sit up all night to read or hear them read. Their thirst for God is insatiable and finally, *finally*, they can discover Him.

The small New Testaments are discovered, of course. Many are burned and destroyed by men furious to be thwarted at their attempts to keep Scripture solely in its original Greek and Hebrew or Latin and away from the common people. Prisons are soon overflowing with Christians. Thousands are executed—just for owning an English New Testament.

Tyndale continues translating and printing until he's caught and arrested in 1535. He spends eighteen months in prison, during which time he works to translate the Old Testament. His translation was never completed because in early October of 1536, William Tyndale, a man whose only crime was to love God's Word, was burned at the stake, while he fervently prayed for God to open the king of England's eyes and allow all to read the Bible.

Our freedom to read Scripture freely and in our own language was bought with the blood of men and women who were passionate for the Bible. The Bibles we hold in our hands and have on our bookshelves are there only because the path was paved with sacrifice, martyrdom, and tremendous courage.

Even today, millions of Christians don't have access to a Bible. Or if they do, they risk their lives on a daily basis by owning one since the Bible is illegal in many countries and extremely difficult to obtain in others.[3] Millions have valued the Bible more than life itself and willingly laid down their own lives for the sake of Scripture.

Will we disgrace their sacrifice through our indifference and complacency? Or will we rise up with a fire for God's Word and treasure our freedom to read it, memorize it, and speak its words of life and truth?

There may come a day when we, too, will have to make a choice between our life and God's Word. What choice will you make then?

What choice will you make today?

— Going Deeper —

1. How many Bibles do you and your family own? How often do you read them?

2. Do you struggle with taking time to read and understand the Bible? Using the tips mentioned, be intentional about giving God the best part of your day and reading the Bible every day.

3. Have you ever studied Scripture before? If so, did you find it helpful? What did you learn?

4. Have you ever tried to memorize Scripture? How did it go? Pick a passage and work on memorizing it this week.

5. Were you aware of the struggle that took place to translate the Bible into English? How does that change your perspective? If you had to choose between your life and the Bible, what would you choose?

PART FOUR

the crux

10

one time around is all we've got

don't waste your life—or your time

Jeremiah Thomas was an All-Star Game football player. He received awards. His team won State. He was handsome, talented, and living his dreams.

But in one year, his life took two drastic turns.

The first happened in the summer of 2017. God captured his heart and ignited a flame of passion for Christ in his soul. God flipped his life and his perspective.

Jeremiah said, "Growing up, I always had one foot in Christ and one foot in the world. I attended church, did Bible study, and ministered with my family, but when I was at school or hanging with friends you couldn't tell that I knew Christ."[1]

All that changed. After that summer, Jeremiah was on fire for God and dedicated to using his life to share the gospel and fight against the "hidden holocaust" of our generation: abortion. He wrote, "I immediately ran to the roar of the battle and began to do ministry outside our local abortion clinic. With my Bible and a handheld microphone, I began sharing the gospel on high school and college campuses."[2]

He still played football—his team won State again in 2017. He played basketball and baseball too. The difference was that now he rejected the apathy and indifference that once marked his teen years. At sixteen, Jeremiah Thomas made a commitment to follow Christ no matter what and fight with all he had for the innocent lives of the unborn.

Then came the second drastic turn.

Basketball season was almost over, and after a game, Jeremiah came home and felt a small pain on his ribs. *Nothing serious,* he thought. He wrapped it up and kept on playing and ministering. But it didn't go away. The pain got worse . . . and worse . . . and worse, until it was unbearable. At first the doctors didn't think anything of it. But as the pain increased, he eventually had a CT scan done. Once again, his life changed drastically.

The pain Jeremiah had been experiencing was linked to cancer. In an article he wrote, Jeremiah expressed his anguish over this discovery.

> My world was turned upside down and inside out. The only thing I could really understand was that I had a tumor in my front chest and it was malignant. I was dying . . .
>
> My dream to play college football was *dead*. My dream to minister was *dead*. We were absolutely blindsided. I was the healthiest I had ever been. I was in my prime! I had so many plans and goals for the year. I couldn't accept the news that I had a malignant tumor, not yet. Not now. Maybe a tumor at seventy years old; I could die at seventy. Not at sixteen.[3]

He didn't understand. Why was this happening when he was so young? When he'd just started living all-out for Christ? When he was in full-time ministry, sharing the gospel, serving, loving, living, and preaching with all he had? Couldn't God use him more if he was healthy and strong? Didn't God see he wanted to dedicate his life to serving Christ and ending abortion?

So why cut it short?

Jeremiah lost everything. He wrote a letter to his generation and posted it on his dad's blog several months after the diagnosis.

> After a few months of cancer and a bunch of different treatments, here I am. I'm lying down in bed, typing this letter. I have lost my hair, my ability to walk, fifty pounds of healthy muscle, the sensation in my legs and back, and my football career. But I haven't lost my faith and hope in God. In fact, my faith in Him has been strengthened.[4]

In the six months that followed his diagnosis, Jeremiah fought valiantly for life.

But not just for *his* life.

He continued fighting for the lives of the unborn. He lived for Christ each fleeting, passing day. He didn't know how much time he had, but he was determined to use every second of it for Jesus. When he was first told that he'd lost the ability to walk, he replied, "Then I'll preach from my wheelchair."[5]

Since his diagnosis, he lived in a state of constant, excruciating pain and devastating loss. He was ridiculed for his outspoken commitment to Jesus. He went through more than I can fathom, but he never lost his faith in our all-powerful, all-good God. In fact, his faith became stronger as he took each day he had and used it for something bigger than himself, even as his body slowly weakened.

He joined the front lines of battle and fought well. He inspired his generation.

He inspired me.

On August 26, 2018, Jeremiah's battle ended and he stood before the One he'd dedicated his life to. He lived well and he died well. My heart broke when I heard the news and I wept for his life and the loss of it, but I praised God for his example and commitment to live all-in for Christ—even in the face of devastating circumstances.

His complete faith in God quiets my heart. It challenges me. How would I spend my days if I knew there was a strong chance I wouldn't be alive much longer? How would I respond? In self-pity? In fear?

Or would I live like Jeremiah, in selfless service and faith?

The truth is Jeremiah didn't ask for his story. He didn't know that just one year after God captured his heart, he'd be fighting for his life, weak and sick.

We don't know our futures either.

We don't know the span of our lives. We can't predict the future. We can't choose much of what happens in life.

All we can choose is how we live each day.

How we live today, knowing it could be our last. How we live each second, each moment.

Are we going to live them for ourselves? Or for something bigger?

Don't Waste Today

I saw something on social media this morning that said: "Use your life for something that will last longer than your Instagram story."

God created us with purpose. His design and plan for each of us is intentional and unique. Our lives matter, because *we* matter greatly to God. There's not a detail too small or insignificant that He doesn't care about it.

And that means how we choose to live matters too. God has a plan for each of us, and part of that plan—no matter what the details look like—means we're accountable for how we use this gift of life He's given us. No matter what course our lives take individually, the main goal and destiny of every Christian is to love God and advance His kingdom. Whether we do that as a missionary or at a nine-to-five job doesn't matter as much as our attitude and desire to live each moment well with the knowledge that our lives are very short but also very precious. Because the truth is, wasting your life started yesterday.

Psalm 90:12 says, "So teach us to number our days, that we may gain a heart of wisdom." Numbering our days reflects the knowledge that every day counts and we can't know the span of our lives. On the same note, Ephesians 5 says, "Be very careful, then, how you live—not as unwise but as wise, making the most of every opportunity, because the days are evil" (vv. 15–16 NIV).

So many of us live each day like it doesn't matter. With no passion. No calling. No service.

Just . . . living. We do the same things. We see the same people. We get stuck in a rut of doing school, having fun, checking social media, and maybe working a job. We're busy, but if we had to pick one meaningful thing we did each day that would last longer than our Instagram story, would we have anything to share?

Deep in our hearts, we all want our lives to count for something bigger than ourselves. We want to look back and see what we've accomplished—the way the world is better or the way we impacted someone's life and made a difference. We're a generation passionate about justice and working to right the wrongs in the world, because we see the wrongs so clearly in our culture. If we're led by Christ, we should be passionate about sharing Him with the people around us.

But here's the thing. Our passion is snuffed out with the day-to-day smothering of distractions. We rationalize that "one day" we'll do something to make a difference. But today? We're too young. Too busy. Too inexperienced. Youth is supposed to be fun, right? Culture tells us to have fun, go for it, and live on the wild side while we're young, dumb, and energetic. We're fed this message on all sides throughout our teen years but then we're still expected to clean up our acts and do something with our lives. As if we're automatically going to turn into responsible, hardworking adults the second we turn twenty-one.

Yeah, right.

But we don't have to wait to make a difference. We can live for Christ *today* and live our lives well *today*. We have incredible, untapped potential. Why would we bottle it up for an elusive "someday"? If you don't want your life ten years from now to look identical to today, then—guess what?—you have to start changing it . . . today. In his book *Thoughts for Young Men*, J. C. Ryle said, "Satan does not care how spiritual your intentions are, or how holy your resolutions, if only they are determined to be done tomorrow."[6]

If you don't want to waste your life, start by not wasting today.

How We Waste Time

But what does this look like practically? It starts with being aware of the activities and mind-sets that steal our time. Here are five common ways we waste our time.

1. Social Media and TV

I have a confession to make: I can't stand social media. Well, actually, I can't stand how addicted I am to it. Social media is, without a doubt, one of the biggest time wasters of our generation. But we don't have to be a slave to it. It has become addictive to us, but we can break free. Start with something small like going one day a week without social media, turning your phone off or turning off notifications, or waiting until after you've eaten breakfast and gotten ready for the day to check social media. I intentionally try to make every Sunday "screenless" by not getting on my phone (unless I have to) and not checking social media at all. As I'm writing this, I'm on day five of a two-week social media break. After a few days of withdrawal, I'm doing okay. I'm learning that I can live without social media. And guess what? You can too. I promise.

The same goes for TV. Statistics don't lie—most people spend an average of four to five hours a day in front of their TV screens.[7] You don't have to go to that extreme to still be wasting time. Think of it this way. How much of your day is "screen time" versus "God time"? If your answer is out of balance, something needs to change. Keep a log of how much time you spend in front of your TV screen (and phone screen), and then evaluate what you could be doing instead.

2. Busyness

We waste time when we're busy. It's true. We're so busy going here and there, doing this and that, and saying yes to every opportunity in our path. But often, we don't do any of it well, because we sometimes use busyness as an excuse to avoid doing what really matters. Are our sports, extracurricular activities, hobbies, and to-do lists keeping us from investing in God and things that have an eternal impact?

Think about what you're doing. Are you doing it well? Is it something that will last? Does it matter in the long run? Does it distract you from something more important? If the answer to any of those questions is yes, then maybe you need to step back from it—or not choose to do it in the first place. Having a jam-packed life doesn't mean it's an impactful life.

3. Not Valuing Minutes

One thousand four hundred and forty. That's how many minutes we have each day. Each one is a precious gift from God. How do you spend yours?

As I said before, Jim Elliot is one of my personal heroes. One thing he understood was the value of a minute. As a college student, he intentionally began every day by reading the Bible. Even when his workload increased, he realized he needed time in Scripture more than ever. He read from the Old Testament in the morning, Psalms at noon, and the New Testament in the evening. Prayer followed, and for Jim, it was constant. Of this time, his wife, Elisabeth, wrote, "He prayed as he walked up to breakfast on campus, or as he stood in line at the dining hall. An odd moment here or there in the day was given to prayer . . . or to memorization of Bible verses which he carried, written on small cards, in his pocket."[8] Jim saturated himself with God's Word and God's presence *every minute of the day*. He was even considered unsociable at times, because he often chose to spend lunchtime with his prayer lists and Scripture cards instead of people. Meanwhile I recently collapsed on the couch with my lunch and rewatched my favorite scenes from *The Greatest Showman*. I'm obviously still learning this lesson.

What would our lives look like if we followed Jim's example? If we valued the spare minutes we have and spent them praying or memorizing Scripture, serving our families and siblings, or not automatically reaching for our phones when we're bored?

Value each minute, because minutes add up to hours, hours add up to days, and days add up to years, and ultimately, a lifetime.

4. Not Resting

At the same time, we need to understand the value of rest. Most people are way off balance when it comes to the rest-versus-work ratio. Some go to a workaholic extreme and never take time to refresh and rejuvenate. Others swing toward the extreme of filling their days with recreation and pursuit of fun. Neither is God's plan. We can value the minutes in our day by knowing *when* and *how* to rest well. Author Jaquelle Crowe Ferris says in her book, *This Changes Everything*, "There is a sharp distinction between laziness and rest. Laziness is selfish time spent in violation of God's command; it's self-absorption and idleness when we are called to work. Rest, on the other hand, is a God-given method of worship that allows us to refresh our hearts and minds. Laziness is bad, but rest is very, very good."[9]

Rest, when it's in balance with how God intended it, is an important tool that can actually help us waste less time. When I'm exhausted and overworked, I don't feel very impactful. I do everything halfheartedly because I'm tired. But when I take time to rest, I have the energy—physical, mental, emotional, and spiritual—to do the work before me well. Rest helps us have a bigger impact, because it gives us the strength to keep working well.

5. Being Self-Focused

We waste time when we live for *us*. When our main goal every day is to accomplish what *we* want to do. Do you want your life to matter? Live it with the goal of glorifying God and serving others.

Sometimes we get so caught up in having to do grand things for God that we forget the most impactful service—loving, praying for, and serving others. Not wasting our lives begins with simply being faithful. Our life impact isn't measured by how many impressive things we do but by how faithful we are each day. One of the biggest time wasters is living solely with the goal of glorifying and pleasing self, and one of the biggest life-changers is living to glorify God and serve people. Living well starts with loving well—God first, others second.

To Live Is Christ

Until recently, one verse in Scripture has always confused me. Philippians 1:21 reads, "For to me, to live is Christ, and to die is gain."

131

This didn't make sense to me. If to die is gain, wouldn't it more correctly be to live is . . . *loss*? To my writerly, grammatically correct mind, the positive of *gain* should be counteracted with the negative of *loss*.

Paul didn't think so. He said to live is *Christ*.

In the verses surrounding this famous declaration, he explained himself, saying that while he'd rather be with Christ, he knew he still needed to live and use his life to serve God. He understood how valuable his life was.

He understood what it meant to not waste your life.

In the verse above, Paul said, "So now also Christ will be magnified in my body whether by life or by death" (Phil. 1:20).

That's when it clicked in my mind. Paul wasn't depreciating the value of life when he said to die was gain; he was outlining the meaning of it.

For centuries, scholars and philosophers have debated and pondered the question, "What is the purpose of life?" The answer is already spelled out in Scripture. The purpose of life is to live for God, know Him, love Him, and share His love with others.

In other words, to live is an opportunity: *Christ* is the opportunity. To die is gain: *Christ* is the gain. So whether we live or die, we revolve around Christ. He is what we live for. He is what we should be willing to die for and who we'll be with forever in eternity. If we live like this, intentionally and purposefully, seeking Him every step of the way, we're in no danger of wasting our lives. Losing them, maybe. Wasting them, never.

The world doesn't understand this. Some people might say we're wasting our youth—and our lives—by not conforming to cultural norms. But if culture says that living all-out for Jesus is wasting my life, then I can think of no higher calling than to "waste my life" for the cause of Christ.

Jeremiah Thomas understood this. Even though he was mocked and insulted for living for Jesus, he didn't succumb to the pressure. While his body was failing, his spirit and faith remained undaunted.

He lived radically for Christ because Christ was the opportunity of his life. Death may have been gain, but until his final moment, Jeremiah committed to not waste even one precious second.[10]

We're not guaranteed tomorrow. All we have is today.

Live it well.

— Going Deeper —

1. What stands out to you in Jeremiah's story? What did you learn from it?

2. How do you think you would react if you knew when your life would end? Would knowing change the way you live? How?

3. What are the biggest time wasters in your life? Which of the five ways we waste time resonated with you the most? How can you start changing that today? Pick one action step and do it.

4. What do you think about the quote: "The purpose of life is to live for God, know Him, love Him, and share His love with others." How would this mind-set change your daily life?

5. What do you think "to live is Christ" means? How can you put that into practice on a daily basis?

11

relationship remodel

how God transforms your relationships

My sister and I have a problem.

Everywhere we go, people think we're twins. At the grocery store, "Are you two girls twins?" At church, "Let me guess . . . are you twins?" Stepping off an elevator, "Oh my goodness! You girls must be twins!"

I'm not joking. People seem to have an unusual fascination with the idea of my sister and I being twins. We've considered getting T-shirts that say, "No, we're not twins," but having the same shirt might add to our twinning vibe. It's even gotten to the point where people think I'm Amanda when she's not there. At a conference recently, someone I didn't know passed me in the hall and said, "Hi, Amanda!" I just smiled and kept walking, thinking, *This is crazy!*

It's become a running joke between us—sisters, pseudo-twins, and best friends. I'm so thankful for my sister and all the precious relationships God has given me. They're an incredible blessing—but they can also be an incredible challenge.

Relationship Trouble?

Let's face it. We have a messy world and messy lives, and we're more than capable of contributing to the messiness—especially in the arena of relationships. Relationships are never easy. They're complicated and confusing, because they're between broken and sinful people. No one is perfect; therefore no relationship is perfect.

So far we've talked about how Christ transforms our lives and how to follow Him wholeheartedly. It sounds great in theory, but there's so much chaos—so many little, nitty-gritty things—you may be wondering, *What does* this *have to do with* that?

How does following Christ change our relationships? How do we approach dating in a God-honoring way? What does obeying God look like when our younger siblings are driving us crazy? What does "honor your parents" really mean?

God cares about our relationships. He created them all—parents and children. Siblings. Friends. Grandparents. Neighbors. Coworkers. And, of course, the tumultuous and exciting world of love, dating, and marriage.

Every relationship is important and comes with its own set of difficulties, rewards, trials, and blessings. Instead of focusing on each individually, I want to talk about four core qualities that are vital in healthy, God-honoring relationships. They can be applied in nearly every relationship we take part in and have the ability to dramatically flip our perspective so it points to Christ.

1. Selflessness

First Corinthians 13 is famously known as the "love chapter" of the Bible. Being a romantic and sappy single, whenever I hear the word *love*, I automatically think of the gushy, gooey, heart-fluttering emotions I encounter in my favorite chick flicks. I find it interesting that one of the most well-known definitions of love doesn't mention emotions at all. In fact, every word Paul used in its description is a verb—an action word. Emotions seem to be completely left out. Let's take a look.

> Love is patient, love is kind. It does not envy, it does not boast, it is not proud. It does not dishonor others, it is not self-seeking, it is not easily angered, it keeps no record of wrongs. Love does not delight in evil but rejoices with the truth. It always protects, always trusts, always hopes, always perseveres. Love never fails. (1 Cor. 13:4–8 NIV)

All of these qualities can be condensed into one phrase: *Love gets over itself.*

To put it more bluntly: *Get over yourself!*

We're the selfie generation. Whether we realize it or not, we've grown up with the mind-set that everything revolves around us. We can have it our way, open happiness, and obey our thirst, because we're worth it (to borrow a few advertising slogans).[1] Our culture has shaped us to think this way, so what I'm about to say next may come as a shock.

It's not all about you. And it never has been.

To have healthy, God-focused relationships, we need to beat back our natural tendencies and cultural mind-sets and get over the idol of *self.*

This is hard, I know. Selfishness is ingrained in our hearts. After all, we live inside ourselves. (That may sound strange, but stick with me.) Because of our extreme closeness with ourselves, it's difficult to truly see other people. It takes effort to feel their hurt, because we're feeling ours. It's not easy to understand their point of view, because we're so busy looking through our own. It's hard to understand their emotions, because we're in such a tangle with our own feelings.

Yet, that's exactly what selfless love calls us to do. To look past ourselves and see—really see—others. It might look like stopping and listening when a friend is struggling instead of just blowing them off, or working an extra shift because your coworker is sick and needs to go home.

It might mean noticing how tired your mom looks and saying thank you for all she does by giving up some of your free time to help her. It may take the form of letting go of anger when your sibling hurts you and forgiving them instead of holding a grudge. Or noticing the girl at school who's always excluded and spending time with her. It might be honoring your future spouse by not casually dating but being intentional in your relationships with the opposite sex because you don't want to mess with others' emotions.

It's loving when we don't feel like loving. Giving when we don't feel like giving. Getting over our own desires, not insisting on our own ways, and reaching out to others. It's in these small areas that self and love collide and make it difficult to live selflessly. But it's also in these small areas that our love is tested and becomes stronger and more like Christ's. It's here that we have the ability to love like Jesus.

The only way we can accomplish this is through the power of the Holy Spirit. Ask for His help. Choose love. Not the glitzy, mushy, emotion-driven love of our society but the transformative, self-giving love of Scripture that is a choice instead of a feeling. To live for Christ, we need to stop living for *us*.

2. Forgiveness

If becoming selfless is hard, mastering forgiveness is even harder. I've been hurt before. Deeply. I'm sure you have too. Forgiveness is letting go of anger and bitterness and learning to love the person that hurt us as Christ loves them. It's one of the hardest things we are asked to do. But we're never more like Jesus than when we forgive.

Because He forgave us.

I recently came face-to-face with the pain and unforgiveness in my heart toward someone who had hurt me. I no longer trusted them. I didn't know what to do with the hurt in my heart and, honestly, I didn't want to face it. I was afraid it would overwhelm me. But God was asking me to forgive.

I wrestled with it. Cried over it. Begged God to help me. And then I had to let it go. I'm still letting it go. But I don't want my hurt to stand between me and God, because He's never let His hurt over my actions stand between us. Instead, He went to the cross to demolish the roadblocks of my sin.

People hurt each other. We're flawed individuals with sinful hearts who are capable of inflicting pain. We mess up on a daily basis, in big areas and small. Forgiveness and repentance are constant requirements for healthy relationships.

Bitterness suffocates love. It's a poison that slowly kills our relationships and can stand between us and God. Once again, Jesus took a radical stand on forgiveness. He said to love our enemies, bless those that curse us, do good to those that hate us, and pray for those who use and persecute us (see Matt. 5:44). Not only did He talk about these things but He also set the standard. Even as people who hated Him were nailing Him to the cross, Jesus's heart broke over their sin, and He cried out to God to forgive them (see Luke 23:34). And He daily forgives us.

Well, yeah, but that's Jesus, we think. But remember: not only was Jesus fully God but He was also fully human. If forgiveness—letting go of even the deepest hurts—was impossible He wouldn't have commanded it. (See Matthew 18:21–35 for Jesus's take on forgiveness.)

Only with God can we find the power to forgive. On our own we can't forgive. But with Christ, we can. It starts with asking for His help. And then, through His power, moving into action. Love and forgiveness are sometimes feelings and then actions, but more often than not, they're actions and then feelings. As we choose to let go of our bitterness, God will fill us with His love and give us the feelings in time.

I don't know who comes to mind when you think about forgiveness. It might be a difficult sibling or a friend who plastered information you told them in secret all over social media. But I think many of us have much more serious and deeper hurts in mind. It might be an adult—or even a peer—who physically or sexually abused you. It might be someone who emotionally abused or bullied you through their words and actions. If that's you, I'm so sorry. I want to be clear that forgiving them does *not* mean you don't hold them accountable for their actions. It doesn't mean you have to stay silent in the face of these kinds of abuse. Forgiveness does *not* mean covering up others' sins and pretending the hurt they caused does not exist. But it does mean letting go of hate and bitterness and releasing both to God. It's okay to be angry and broken by the hurts and injustices people inflict upon us. But it's not okay to let that anger harden our hearts and stand in the way of our relationship with God.

Is there bitterness and unforgiveness in your heart that's damaging your relationships or hindering your walk with God? I challenge you to start the process of letting it go today. It's not easy and I don't want to simplify your pain. It's a process that begins by asking God to help you. Know that however deep the hurt may be, Jesus knows. Your pain hurts Him too. And that's what gives us the ability to let go and truly forgive.

3. Humility

Real talk here. Our generation is not exactly known for our humility. Something about being young and on top of the world, with our whole lives ahead of us, equals a recipe for pride with a side of arrogance.

I've fought against pride. Oh, have I ever. It's always a battle, and what I've realized is that pride is one of the greatest relationship destroyers. There's a remedy for it though, and it's found in Philippians 2:3–4. Paul was writing about having unity and being of one mind in church and community. Then he said, "Let nothing be done through selfish ambition or conceit, but in lowliness of mind let each esteem others better than himself. Let each of you look out not only for his own interests, but also for the interests of others."

Pride (selfish ambition and conceit) equals division. Humility (lowliness of mind) equals unity. And unified relationships are strong relationships.

Pride puts all the focus on us. When we're proud and arrogant, we become an island unto ourselves. We try to be the best, the greatest, the most popular, the top of our class, or at least the best in our clique. Pride is rooted in insecurity and insecurity is rooted in self-focus.

Humility, on the other hand, puts the focus on God and others. It's selflessness's cousin. It seeks to deflect praise to whom it belongs—God. When we're humble, we know we need others and can't do it alone.

Read a little further in Philippians and you'll find our model for humility—Jesus Himself.

> Let this mind be in you which was also in Christ Jesus, who, being in the form of God, did not consider it robbery to be equal with God, but made Himself of no reputation, taking the form of a bondservant and coming in the likeness of men. And being found in appearance as a man, He humbled Himself and became obedient to the point of death, even the death of the cross. (Phil. 2:5–8)

This says that Jesus, who was completely equal with God, humbled Himself. He didn't brag. Yes, He was fully God and "did not consider it robbery to be equal with God," but His goal wasn't praise or applause. Dying on the cross was the most despised form of execution, but Jesus humbled Himself that low.

And because of His humility, unity was restored between God and humanity.

And again we see that humility equals unity.

Just like selflessness and forgiveness, humility is only possible through Christ's strength. When we're rooted in God, we don't need to prove ourselves to feel loved or accepted because we know we already are. Timothy Keller summarizes humanity well in his book *The Reason for God*,

> When we discern Jesus moving toward us and encircling us with an infinite, self-giving love, we are invited to put our lives on a whole new foundation. . . . Then we don't need to prove ourselves to others. We won't need to use others to bolster our fragile sense of pride and self-worth. And we will be enabled to move out toward others as Jesus has moved toward us.[2]

4. Purity

Here's the segment you've all been waiting for. The romantic relationships part. As fascinated as we are with this topic, it's also a topic where our flesh gets in the way big time. Just this morning I was talking with a girl who wanted to argue with me about flirting. She said flirting isn't mentioned in the Bible. She's right. But purity is.

That's the one thing that should guide our relationships with the young men and women we encounter. Purity in our minds. Purity in our actions. Purity in our bodies. Purity in every interaction we have, romantic relationship or not.

Purity starts in the heart. If our heart isn't right, our actions don't stand a chance. It's closely connected with respect. If we respect those around us, we'll desire to treat them honorably and purely. We'll be careful to ensure that our interactions are pure and guard our minds so our thoughts are honorable. Selflessness shows up again. We're responsible not just for guarding our own purity but also for responding to that of the other person. Purity matters to me because Jesus matters to me. I don't want to find out one day that I was so interested in fulfilling my own desires that I hurt my brothers in Christ. That's why I strive for purity. For me but also for them.

I know what a struggle this is. I've wrestled with impure thoughts, unfulfilled desires, confusing relationships, and heartache. It would be easier if God gave us a step-by-step guide to know how to handle our emotions, embrace purity, and honor Him. But I think part of the reason He didn't give us a relationship rule book is because He wants us to seek Him above all else.

The reason we have so much confusion and impurity in our relationships isn't because our society has an excess of love but a lack of pure, Christlike love. Infatuation heavily permeates our society and infatuation isn't love.

The kind of love godly relationships need is the kind that respects and guards purity and intentionally avoids situations where temptation might grow. Guys, please love the girls around you enough to give of yourselves to protect and guard their hearts. Girls, let's love the young men we know as brothers in Christ first and foremost.

Seek God for strength to choose purity. Seek Him for wisdom in how to act. Seek Him when waiting and patience is tough. Seek Him when you know your attitude is wrong and when you've made mistakes. Seek Him when you don't understand your emotions. After all, He designed relationships and knows how they're supposed to work. And above all, pursue the true purity of heart brought on through a passionate love for Christ.

A Note about Friendship

One of the amazing things about relationships is that God can use them to enrich our relationship with Him. Have you ever met someone so kind, genuine, and filled with Christ's love that you walk away from them thinking, *Wow, I want to be like that*? I have!

I'm always challenged and inspired when I interact with people like that. Their witness is incredibly powerful and influential.

Unfortunately, the opposite can also be true. Instead of drawing us toward Jesus, people can (even unintentionally) draw us away from God. That's why it's so important to be wise and careful about who we choose to be our best friends, because their influence over us will be strong. I wholeheartedly believe we're called to share our faith with, and even befriend, unbelievers and weak Christians and be a witness to them. However, to grow nearer to Christ, our closest, heart-level friends should be those who are strong in their faith and able to strengthen and build us up, and vice versa.

Over the years, I've had to step away from friendships that were harming my relationship with Christ. I saw changes in my life because of their influence and knew it wasn't what God wanted. I didn't consider myself better than them by any means, but I knew I wasn't going to grow if I remained in that circle of friendship. On the other hand, I have a friend named Tabitha who inspires me to love God more and has helped me grow stronger in my faith.

I encourage you to seek out wise and godly friends. Pray for God to bring people like this into your life. If you feel like one of your friends is weakening your faith or causing you to compromise your values, I challenge you to prayerfully and wisely consider if remaining in the current level of closeness is what God wants you to do. Friends can lift you up or pull you down. Choose friends that challenge you to read your Bible, pray for you, and inspire you to follow Jesus. A friendship like that can be one of the most influential aspects of your walk with God and one you'll never regret.

Relationships like God Intended

Relationships *are* messy. And complicated. But there's another thing about relationships we can't forget.

They're God's good gift.

Relationships became confusing, complicated, and riddled with pain after sin entered our world, but God has a better plan in mind. In a world of division, jealousy, bullying, hatred, and anger, God still has a better vision.

It's a vison of unity and selflessness. Of love and kindness. We see glimpses of this better way when we choose to put Jesus first in our relationships. One day it will come to pass completely when Jesus returns, but until then we keep on creating little pockets of heaven on earth when we offer grace instead of wrath. Forgiveness instead of hatred. Purity in a world of impurity.

When we take the time to love instead of judge. When we sit down with a friend and offer a listening ear and shoulder to cry on. When we honor our parents and pray for those around us. When we get over ourselves and live all-out for Christ.

If we choose this radical lifestyle, we would be living, breathing examples of the power of Christ. Echoes of the One who died for us. The heartbeat of Jesus's love in action.

It's hard work, no doubt about it. It requires self-sacrifice and time. A lot of love and maybe a few tears. But it's the kind of love the world needs to see. The love of Christ in us.

— Going Deeper —

1. Rate yourself on each of the four core qualities of a healthy relationship. On a scale of 1 to 10, how are you doing on each? (1 is terrible, 10 is great.) Which is the hardest and why?

2. Why do you think selflessness is one of the most important aspects of a healthy relationship? How can you practically practice selflessness today?

3. Think of the last time you were hurt. Have you forgiven the person who hurt you? Why or why not?

4. When it comes to romantic relationships, what's the biggest struggle you face? Seek God in that struggle and ask for His help to love like He loves.

5. Why do you think friendships can be so powerful? Have you ever had a friend who drew you closer to God? Have you ever had a friend who led you to compromise?

12

social media, tv, technology, oh my!

giving God control of your media and entertainment

Have you ever thought about how much our lives are dominated by technology and media?

We have dozens of apps on our phones that help us keep in touch, save money, and stay fit. We use computers to do work or play games. We use TVs to watch shows, hear the news, and entertain and educate ourselves. Having a social media account has been likened to having a full-time job because we check our devices dozens of times a day.

It's especially true of teenagers. We're the iGen. We've never known anything else. Media is an inherent part of our lives, like eating, sleeping, and breathing. We don't think about it. We just do it.

The fact that it's such a big part of our lives means we have to be more intentional and careful than ever to use media wisely as

Christ followers. As I've grown in my walk with God, I've wondered, *How do I worship God when I'm watching TV? What does serving Him look like when I'm scrolling social media? Does God care about my "media life"?* In our media-soaked world, it's doubtless we'll encounter questions like these as we strive to honor God.

Two Lies We Believe About Media

Before we move forward, let's debunk two common lies we believe when it comes to things like the time we spend on our social media accounts and watching our favorite TV programs.

LIE #1: *It's Just Entertainment—It Doesn't Affect Me*

TRUTH #1: *Everything We Put in Front of Us Affects Us*

Yesterday, a Christian I know attempted to defend her reasons for reading a clearly unbiblical (but culturally popular) book series. Her reason? *It's just entertainment.*

I think we'd all agree that there's such a thing as healthy food and junk food, and what we put into our bodies affects our health. If so, why is it unfathomable to think that what we put before our eyes, and inside our brains, affects our mental, emotional, and spiritual health? We think it's "just entertainment," but entertainment is a powerful force. We're swept away by story. We move to rhythm and beat. We laugh at funny memes posted on social media. Entertainment has the ability to take us to a different world, change our mood, and make us experience new and exciting things.

And we think it doesn't affect us?!

In *A Practical Guide to Culture*, Brett Kunkle and John Stonestreet share a few of the arguments most people have about entertainment: "The purpose of music, movies, and TV shows is to deliver fun, enjoyment, and leisure. Entertainers entertain; they don't try to change the world. Or so the cultural lie goes."[1]

Don't think you're being affected?

147

Have you ever cried during a movie? Laughed? Ever shared a funny video with friends and found yourself giggling over it hours after watching it?

You're being affected.

We all are. Media is one of the strongest culture dominators.

The lie of "just entertainment" doesn't work. We have to be careful about what we're watching, listening to, reading, looking at, and following. We have to be able to discern if something is affecting us for good or bad and if it glorifies God or sends unbiblical messages. Even if our friends think it's fine, we need to determine it for ourselves, with the guidance of Scripture.

LIE # 2: *Everyone's Watching (or Listening, Reading, Following) It— So I Can Too*

TRUTH #2: *Christ Followers Don't Go with the Flow*

In areas like media, it seems we're all falling into the current of what's trending and popular. This shows up in how eager we are to watch that new movie a friend recommended and why we're so interested in following celebrities' lives. We have a terrible case of FOMO—fear of missing out. But what exactly are we afraid of missing out on?

Our society at large is going down a path I don't want to follow. That includes media choices. My mom often reminds me to be wary of anything that has a mass following—things that the world seems to approve of and applaud. Jesus said we're not to be of the world and that the world will hate us, because we live differently. And if we live differently, we can't love what the world loves (see John 15:18–19).

That absolutely includes what choices we make in our media and entertainment use. Christ followers don't go with the flow. We don't accept what the majority accepts. Just because other people do, it doesn't make it right. Often it makes it wrong. We need to think long and hard, dig into Scripture, and make our entertainment choices according to what God thinks and says.

The Media Filter

At the same time we're being wise and discerning, we also don't want to be legalistic. A legalistic approach might look like banning all social media, movies that aren't expressly Christian, songs that aren't hymns, or even throwing away our TVs and smartphones. God may call some to do that if any of those things are hindering their relationship with Him, but He may not necessarily require that from all of us. This is where discernment comes in.

There are certain types of media and entertainment that aren't explicitly Christian that I personally love. They may not have a Christian message but so long as they're not damaging to my witness as a Christ follower or harmful to my relationship with God, I can enjoy them in moderation.

I love cute and clean rom-coms (even though they're sometimes atrociously cheesy!), have several favorite British shows, love well-done dramas, and am nerdy enough to adore old black-and-white movies. I try to be discerning in my choices—in music, books, and how I use social media as well.

This is where it can get confusing and sticky. I can't tell you what you should or shouldn't watch, listen to, read, or follow. Some things are clearly off-limits, but others are harder to determine. To help you with your decisions, I've created a media filter with five questions to help you determine if your media choices are helping or hindering your walk with God.

1. Why Am I Using It?

With every form of media, it's important to understand the *why*. Why are we on social media? Why is it necessary to post that? Why are we watching this movie or show or listening to this music?

Is it because we find it uplifting and encouraging? Because all our peers are doing it? Because it'll make us feel like we fit in? This goes back to being able to think about media and entertainment through the lens of Scripture.

Sometimes our *whys* may be valid but not appropriate. Yes, we may find that show fun and have a very clear *why*, but that doesn't change the fact that it's inappropriate and contradicts Scripture. Yes, that may be a hilarious thing to post on social media, but that doesn't change the fact that the picture shows too much skin and the caption pushes the boundaries of purity. This may sound harsh, but we need to clearly get our *whys* in order and make sure they're also in line with God's Word.

2. Does It Overtake My Mind and Time?

Even good things can become obsessions, and if something is overtaking our minds, it doesn't matter how good or fun it is. Obsessions distract us from Christ and our purpose to live for Him. We can't live wholeheartedly for God if we're obsessing over creating a picture-perfect Instagram wall or constantly stalking our favorite YouTuber. If it's overtaking our minds, there's no doubt that it's also overtaking our time. As we've discussed, media can be a huge time waster if we're not careful.

Ask yourself this question, Does it overtake my mind and time?

3. Does It Damage My Worldview?

Media is overflowing with subtle messages. Those that create content know how powerful it is. Songs and TV shows promote a hookup culture that doesn't value commitment, integrity, and abstinence. Celebrities promote LGBTQ and pro-choice agendas and gender-fluid worldviews. Social media users spread their opinions for all the world to see, and much of it doesn't align with what God says. Suicides have increased because of cyberbullying,[2] excessive screen-time,[3] the devaluation of life in many books, movies, and YouTube channels,[4] and because we battle depression and feelings of hopelessness and insignificance more than any other generation. This heartbreaking cycle needs to stop.

One afternoon, when I was babysitting two little boys, they turned on the TV and flipped the channel to the Cartoon Network. Within a few minutes, I was shocked at the subtle (and not-so-subtle) messages on display. Lust, greed, anger, revenge, selfishness, and a myriad of other messages were fed to a captive, unaware audience.

I've felt the same way sitting in a darkened movie theater, squirming in my seat as the previews played. Even if I was there to see a Christian film, and even if the previews weren't "that bad," I've literally sensed the presence of evil and a demonic force emanating from the screen at times. Be warned—there is more at play than what meets the eye. Satan uses media and we don't simply wrestle against flesh and blood (see Eph. 6:12). With these kinds of messages on offer, from the Cartoon Network to the big screen, we need to be vigilant and ruthless in our evaluation of what we set before us.

We can't be careless about the worldviews and opinions we're allowing on our phones, in our earbuds, and on our TVs. We can't just say "I can handle it" or "It's not that bad." Like the proverbial frog in the pot, we're becoming desensitized to these messages because they're all around us, slowly creeping in. And they don't have to be overt to be powerful. More often than not, they're hidden beneath the surface.

We shouldn't be ignorant but we also shouldn't allow our media and entertainment use to become saturated with the opinions of the world. Doing so will allow the opinions of the world to saturate us.

4. Does It Contradict Scripture?

The Bible doesn't have anything specific to say about social media or TV. But for the record, it does have a lot to say about how we should live. Which is why this is the most important question on the list.

The Bible paints many vivid pictures between light and darkness. One of them is found in Galatians 5. Let's see what it has to say:

> Now the works of the flesh are evident, which are: adultery, fornication, uncleanness, lewdness, idolatry, sorcery, hatred, contentions, jealousies, outbursts of wrath, selfish ambitions, dissensions, heresies, envy, murders, drunkenness, revelries, and the like. (vv. 19–21)

Did you just read what I just read? Adultery, hatred, jealousy, outbursts of wrath, envy? Whoa, I think Galatians just wrote the script for the TV show I saw a minute of in the doctor's office the other day.

Now for the flip side. "But the fruit of the Spirit is love, joy, peace, longsuffering, kindness, goodness, faithfulness, gentleness, self-control" (vv. 22–23).

Total difference, isn't it? You see, we don't have to watch those terrible, low-budget TV shows to consume media that contradicts Scripture. It's everywhere, and often, it's extremely popular. Our frame isn't verses 20 through 21 (that's obvious enough). It's verses 22 and 23. Now those standards are harder to measure up to. We're not supposed to skim over the first two verses before we post something on social media and think, *Okay, no murders or drunkenness or idolatry in this post. I guess it's good!* Rather we should think, *Is this loving? Does it show kindness? Does it portray Christ's faithfulness? Is it gentle? Am I being self-controlled?*

On a side note, it's important to realize there's a difference between something *portraying* sin and something *glorifying* it. Sin is alive and well in our world. It's impossible to escape the realities of life and enclose ourselves in a sin-free bubble. We can learn deep truths and scripturally sound lessons through the mistakes of others and the consequences faced. The caveat is whether or not it's portrayed as wrong or whether it's lifted up as an example to follow. The former we can learn from; the latter we can be influenced by.

This applies to the movies we watch, the songs we listen to, and just about everything else in our lives. It doesn't mean that all our media forms need to have an explicit Christian message but rather that they don't tear down the messages of Scripture. The question is, Does it pull me away from Christ or confuse what He's teaching me? Does it glorify sin as something to be emulated or does it warn against the consequences and point me to truth?

When you're unsure about a media choice, ask yourself: does it contradict Scripture?

5. Is It Uplifting and Pure?

The book of Philippians gives us another list to follow. This one challenges us to consider what we're thinking about.

> Finally, brethren, whatever things are true, whatever things are noble, whatever things are just, whatever things are pure, whatever things are lovely, whatever things are of good report, if there is any virtue and if there is anything praiseworthy—meditate on these things. (Phil. 4:8)

Paul told the Philippians to filter everything through this list. While I don't think the Philippians were debating about technology, we can learn a lot from this filter. Are our social media posts true and noble and just? Are the things we watch when we collapse in front of the TV pure and lovely and of good report? Are they virtuous and praiseworthy? We can't meditate on pure and holy things if we're consistently filling our minds with dirty and impure things. It's just not possible.

There's one thing I want to focus on here. Even though it's completely obvious, I feel I can't ignore it. It's one of the darkest forms of media and one that has lasting and costly consequences. I'm talking about pornography.

You don't even have to think about it before you know that pornography doesn't make it through the Philippians filter. But it's something that more and more people are struggling with. Especially teens. And girls, it's not just a guy's problem. I've known young women battling this addiction as well.

I don't know your background with topics like this. You may be absolutely shocked by it or this may hit a little too close to where you're at right now. But I do know that pornography has absolutely no place in the life of a committed Christ follower. And even though people think it's a personal matter, or it doesn't affect them, or it's not an addiction, or that "this will be the last time," those are all lies.

Worst of all, pornography fuels a horrific industry—*sex trafficking*. Nearly five million people are enslaved and abused in this industry and more than one million children are victims each year.[5] When we view pornography, we're abusing and stripping the dignity of these victims. We need to fight against this horror—not feed it. And it starts with us saying no. We need to wake up to the fact that it's serious and has consequences that are real and lasting, more harmful than we could ever comprehend.

But you can *be free from it.*

Christopher Witmer, the editor-in-chief of TheRebelution .com, shares his story of breaking free from pornography and says,

> One of the biggest lies a follower of the resurrected Jesus could believe is there is no complete victory over sexual sin . . . We may always wrestle against the temptation, but I believe with all my heart we can walk in complete freedom, even to the point of not even desiring lust. What did Jesus die for if it doesn't include victory over sin? Has God lost the power which raised Jesus from the dead? . . . Jesus's power is strong. His grace endless. His victory

complete. If Jesus can be raised from the dead, can't the gospel also free us from lust?[6]

This is a young man who knows the struggle. He's been there. But he also knows that it's possible to be free, because Christ has set us free from sin. Because of that, even if you've battled this in the past—or are battling it now—there doesn't have to be shame in your future. Through Christ, you are a conqueror and He covers your shame with His blood.

If you're battling this, please seek out someone trustworthy to tell. Satan wants us to keep our struggles hidden, because he can have power over us in the dark. So bring it into the light. Tell someone. Find accountability. Get counseling and take action. Put filters on your devices and have people who are allowed full access to your phone and computer. Fight against the injustice of pornography. Take steps toward freedom—for you *and* those enslaved—and walk in the freedom Jesus bought on the cross.

In all of our media usage, let's strive for purity.

Media Done Right

I know I just said some pretty countercultural things. They're not politically correct—but I'd rather be biblically correct.

That's our goal. It's not legalism. It's not to create a list of dos and don'ts. It's simply to follow Jesus.

So should we ditch all forms of media?

I can't answer that for everyone. Instead of offering a legalistic approach, I'd encourage a countercultural approach. Media has been a tool for evil in the hands of many, but it doesn't have to be. Romans 12:2 says, "And do not be conformed to this world, but be transformed by the renewing of your mind."

Are we conforming more than we're transforming? Does media have more of our attention than the Word of God?

Jesus invades and changes every part of our lives, and our media usage is not exempt from the overhaul. We're representatives of Christ and how we use media should reflect that.

If we choose to use media, let's use it differently than the world. To encourage instead of discourage. To promote purity instead of impurity. Build up instead of tear down. Be others-focused instead of self-focused. To be wise and discerning and not to be afraid to stand out from the crowd.

— Going Deeper —

1. What are your favorite media formats? Are they hindering your relationship with Christ?
2. What lies have you believed when it comes to media and entertainment?
3. Do you think God cares about your social media and technology usage? Why or why not?
4. Pick two of your favorite forms of media (e.g., a favorite movie, music artist, etc.) and run them through the media filter. Ask yourself the five questions and answer honestly.
5. If they didn't make it through the filter, what are you going to do about it? How can you take practical steps to cleanse your life of impure media influences?

PART FIVE

the commission

13

go out and speak out

we gotta spread this love riot

His name was Pedro, but they all called him "Papa Pete." He was thirty-eight when he embarked on a journey to discover what was missing in his life. Desperate and seeking, his journey led him to a church parking lot and to a man bold enough to reach out to him.

It also led him to Jesus.

From that moment on, Pedro's life changed drastically. I never met him, but I heard story after story from his daughter, Jocelyn, my mom's close friend.

After Jesus captured his heart, Pedro's life goal could be condensed into four words: *tell people about Jesus.* For forty years, he did for others what one man had done for him. From preaching in prison cells to church planting in Uruguay, and eventually sharing the gospel from a hospital bed in Pennsylvania, Pedro told everyone he could about the God who saved him.

He had a goal to share the gospel with at least one person every day. Genuine love for others and a passion for Christ spurred him on day after day. He was a man who would give the shirt off his back for another. One afternoon, while on a mission trip to Haiti, he literally did just that.

Walking the streets, looking for someone to talk to, Pedro came across a shirtless man sitting by the side of the road. There was only one thing to do—give him the shirt off his own back, sit down, and start talking about Jesus.

Some might scoff at how relentless Pedro was in sharing Christ. They might say he was too bold or that he took it too seriously. But he knew that wasn't true. God called him to preach the gospel.

And He calls each of us to do the same.

The Greatest Commission

Jesus gave us a commission. He equipped us with the Holy Spirit, gave us a voice, and commanded us to go.

Before He ascended into heaven, Jesus gave us one last challenge and assignment: "Go into all the world and preach the gospel" (Mark 16:15).

Think about that for a minute. God entrusted us—*us!*—to be messengers of the greatest message ever heard: the news of salvation and eternal life. I know God today because other people were faithful enough to preach the gospel. You know God today because someone shared Him with you as well.

Aren't you glad they did?

Now it's our responsibility to go out and share the gospel. There's debate inside Christian circles about how to actually go about it though. Some people go for the more subtle "preach the gospel always and, if necessary, use words"[1] approach. Others have "missionary friendships." Still others are bolder, like Pedro, and share the gospel with anyone who will listen—and even some who won't. Some people go into different countries, while others think of their own neighborhood as a mission field.

God can use all those methods, but boiled down, the definition of sharing the gospel can be condensed into the four words that were Pedro's life motto: tell people about Jesus.

For that, all you need is a testimony of grace, a heart full of love, and a voice bold enough to speak out.

Love > Judgment

Occasionally during the summer, you can find a group of people standing on the street corners of my town. They hold signs that read, "Repent or Perish!" and "Will you go to Heaven or Hell?" They loudly preach to anyone who passes by, handing out pamphlets with the same messages. Their words are meant to scare people into giving their lives to Christ. They've turned the gospel—the *Good News*—into a fear-driven message of very *bad news*.

Their message does contain truth—repenting saves us from spiritually perishing and we should think about the reality of heaven and hell—but they leave out the most powerful part of the story: *Jesus's love*.

Jesus never asked us to share the gospel like that. He certainly didn't in His own ministry. He didn't stand on the street corner and scream condemnation at people. He went into their homes and ate with them. He didn't use scare tactics and threats. He told the woman caught in adultery that she was forgiven and that she should go and sin no more. He didn't hit people over the head with a list of rules but actually rebuked the hypocritical rule followers and Pharisees. He spoke hard truths and revealed areas of sin. He didn't mince words. He challenged complete and radical obedience. But He genuinely loved those He spoke to. Matthew 9:36–37 says, "But when He saw the multitudes, He was moved with compassion for them, because they were weary

161

and scattered, like sheep having no shepherd. Then He said to His disciples, 'The harvest truly is plentiful, but the laborers are few.'"

We're the laborers, but I don't think we're as moved with compassion as Jesus is for the harvest.

That's where sharing the gospel needs to start—with our love. If we don't have love, we're compromising the message. If we don't have love, we're probably not sharing it at all.

Authentic Witnessing 101

Authentic witnessing begins with our own relationship with Christ. The only way we can ever love others enough to want to share Jesus with them is to overflow with His love. Love for God directly correlates with love for others, and our love for Him leads us to desire that they experience Him too.

I was recently chatting with my sister, and she shared something profound. She said, "Witnessing is like introducing people to your best friend. If Jesus really is your best friend, you'll want to tell people about Him."

That's step one. Step two is letting our love for God, and His love for us, change the way we view the people around us—being moved with compassion, like Jesus, for the "multitudes" we know. Caring, like Jesus, for both their lives and their souls.

This is such a vital part of following Christ. And honestly, it's one of the hardest. It involves getting over ourselves in order to see people the way God sees them.

The girl in school no one likes? God doesn't see her as rude, arrogant, or stuck-up. He sees the heart behind the mask, with all its brokenness, struggles, and tears, and He longs for her to know Him and His restoring power.

The man who lives across the street and is always complaining and irritable? God doesn't think of him as mean and grouchy. He sees his past. He sees his hurt and loneliness, and He wants to transform his future into one of healing and eternity spent in His holy presence.

Whoever it is, God sees them in truth. We only see the external but God sees the internal and, believe it or not, loves them in spite of it. Wants to save them in spite of it. The same way He loves *you* in spite of your failures and brokenness. The same way He's offered salvation to *you*.

Once we understand God's love for a person, we'll want them to meet the God who's given us the grace we never deserved. Every person we encounter has an eternity before them, and only the message of Jesus can redeem their eternity. Will we share it? Will we love them enough to care? It takes a lot of prayer and help from God and the Holy Spirit. But it *is* possible.

That leads to step three: sharing the love.

This can be manifested in a hundred different ways: Praying with or for someone. Asking questions and learning that person's story. Boldly standing up for truth and sharing the amazing news of the cross. Standing alongside people no one else associates with. Walking beside the broken. Providing resources someone needs—encouragement, finances, food, or maybe just your time. Letting them know it's Jesus that leads you to do it all and makes you different and it's Jesus that can change their lives too. Remember, the definition of sharing the gospel is simply telling others about Jesus and the path of forgiveness.

You should also keep in mind that it's important to be sensitive to the Holy Spirit's leading when we share the gospel. We don't know the story of each individual we encounter, but God does. He knows what they need to hear and how to reach them. If we learn to be open to the Holy Spirit's guidance, we'll be much more effective in our witness. With some people you'll have an open door to verbally and clearly present the gospel. With those people, be bold enough to communicate the story of salvation. With everyone, let your life spell out that story. Like the British evangelist Rodney "Gypsy" Smith said, "There are five Gospels: Matthew, Mark, Luke, John, and the Christian. Most people will never read the first four."[2]

Pursue Justice (but Prioritize the Gospel)

One thing I love about our generation is our passion for justice and working to right the wrongs in the world. Many of us are social justice warriors who fight human trafficking, poverty, hunger, abortion, and racism. These are important issues and ones we should work to see changed.

But there's a danger I fear we sometimes succumb to. I fear we separate sharing the gospel and fighting for justice and equality into two categories. We elevate one over the other, instead of understanding that they actually go hand in hand.

It's vital that we, as Christ followers, take up the baton of truth and work to push back the evil shrouding our world. There's so much brokenness, pain, and suffering, and my heart aches because of it. I believe God aches over the suffering of His creation as well. And what's more? I believe the heart of the church is called to bleed and break on behalf of the oppressed.

In Matthew 25, Jesus gave us a challenge.

> Then the King will say to those on His right hand, "Come, you blessed of My Father, inherit the kingdom prepared for you from the foundation of the world: for I was hungry and you gave Me food; I was thirsty and you gave Me drink; I was a stranger and you took Me in; I was naked and you clothed Me; I was sick and you visited Me; I was in prison and you came to Me.... Assuredly, I say to you, inasmuch as you did it to one of the least of these, My brethren, you did it to Me." (vv. 34–36, 40)

Jesus's heart is for the hurting. So much so that He equates serving *them* with serving *Him*. The poverty-stricken and malnourished child equals the least of these. The innocent, unborn baby about to be aborted equals the least of these. The girl cruelly enslaved and daily forced to sell her body equals the least of these. The homeless on the streets of your town equals the least of these. The single parent next door struggling to feed the kids equals the least of these.

This is the true call of love and justice. To reach out to the "least of these" wherever we may find them—in our neighborhood or at the grocery store, on the street corners or in the slums or across the world in another country. We're called to feed, clothe, and care for them, granting freedom and equality.

If you're not already involved in practically helping and serving, I challenge you to take action. What are you passionate about? What breaks your heart? What do you see around you that breaks God's heart? Don't ignore that pull of passion in your soul because you're too busy or it feels like too big of a problem. Whether it's a passion to feed starving children, a desire to see abortion ended, or a soul-deep fervency to free captives of modern-day slavery, God has lit a fire in your heart. Don't ignore it. *Share it.*

Over the years, I've raised money to fight modern-day slavery and spoken publically about the evils of human trafficking. I've volunteered at local pregnancy centers and pro-life organizations, working to protect the lives of the unborn.

I challenge you to use your sphere of influence and tell the kids at your school or youth group about the problems you want to see fixed. Tell your pastor or youth leader and get your church involved. Write about it. Talk about it on social media. Speak out for those who can't speak for themselves (see Prov. 31:8). Raise money for organizations that serve the broken and oppressed and volunteer where you can. Take one day a week to help out at a local pregnancy center or pray outside an abortion clinic. Or keep bags in your car filled with a Bible and some food to pass out to the homeless on the streets. Maybe you have a dream to help poverty-stricken children overseas, but you feel stuck in your small town. Don't wait—start there. Poverty and brokenness can be found in our own cities and neighborhoods, and there are usually organizations working to meet those needs. And if there isn't, maybe you should start one! There are so many ways you can begin to make a difference right here. Right now.

But in our works of justice, let's not forget what people really need: Jesus. We can free the slaves, feed the hungry, give money to the poor, but if we don't give them Jesus, we leave them just as enslaved, starving, and destitute as before. Jesus linked the spiritual needs of people with their physical needs and cared for both. He calls us to do the same. I love what Jaquelle Crowe Ferris says:

> We need justice operated out of gospel love . . . [Jesus] provided physically for the poor while telling them about the spiritual riches they could have in him. He drew water for the thirsty and told them about the Living Water that could eternally satisfy. He served food to the hungry and preached about the Bread of Life. He cared about children and orphans and offered the opportunity to be God's children. Jesus didn't ignore people's physical suffering, but he prioritized their eternal suffering.[3]

A life of compassion and acts of love are not a substitute for the gospel. We're not exempt from verbally communicating the gospel because we're social justice warriors. That's an excuse and a direct insult to the sacrifice Jesus made on the cross. Our love must clearly shine through in our lives before, after, and as we share the gospel or the message will be diminished. The Bible says, "How shall they believe in Him of whom they have not heard? And how shall they hear without a preacher? . . . So then faith comes by hearing, and hearing by the word of God" (Rom. 10:14, 17). People come to know Christ because they hear the gospel.

While this world may never be fully mended, broken people can still be healed by the power of Christ. We might not be able to save the planet, but Jesus is still in the business of saving souls.

We're called to be preachers of the good news. God called us to be agents of His truth and givers of His love. Sharing the gospel is serious business and we need to realize its importance.

Yes, It's Hard

Sharing the gospel is the hardest part of following Jesus for me. As I've said before, I'm an introvert who doesn't enjoy going outside my comfort zone, and sharing the gospel is way outside my comfort zone.

My church once did a sermon series on evangelism, and one message especially convicted me. The pastor of my church challenged us to reach out and love, asking us how often we brush people off by our silence and inaction. "Silence is the enemy of truth," he said. It hit me hard, and I realized I didn't have a witnessing problem or an introvert problem—I had a love problem. I was so wrapped up in me and my anxieties that I didn't love others like Jesus does.

I wish I could say I was a witnessing dynamo after that Sunday. That all my fears and anxieties vanished and I never missed another opportunity to share Christ's love again. Unfortunately, that's not what happened. Even now, years later, I struggle. I know I've missed opportunities since then, but I've also taken opportunities. I've been bolder and braver. I've said yes.

One time in particular stands out to me. Several years after my mom and sister stopped volunteering in the prison ministry, I felt God's spirit nudging me to go. So I started to meet with female inmates every other week, sharing the gospel and praying for them. Every morning before I went, a wave of fear and anxiety hit me. The results seemed minimal at best. It was discouraging to spend hours beforehand wracked with anxiety, only to leave feeling like I'd wasted my time.

Then I met Bethany.

One of the first things I noticed was her *brokenness*. It emanated from her, more noticeable than her orange prison uniform or the acne she seemed so embarrassed about. She was about my age, but heaviness surrounded her as if she'd already lived several lifetimes and carried the heartache of them all.

She attended my group early on and kept her gaze down almost the entire time. When I stepped through the final security gate two weeks after our first meeting, I was surprised to see her waiting in the hall with three other inmates.

We moved into the room designated for classes and programs and sat around the plastic table. She stayed quiet as I chatted with the other three girls. Taking a deep breath, I began sharing the lesson I'd prepared.

"Do you know what the word *gospel* means?" I asked.

"Yeah, sure," one of the more talkative girls replied. "It means like, um, southern gospel music, right?"

I smiled. "Great guess! But actually, the word *gospel* means 'good news.'"

"Wow, really?" she exclaimed. "That's really cool!"

I glanced at Bethany. She kept her gaze focused somewhere between the floor and the edge of the plastic table. My heart ached for her.

I prayed, *God, please guide me. Reach out to her.*

"I know, I thought that was pretty cool too. Especially since the gospel—the story of Jesus Christ and how He died to save us from our sins—is literally the best news ever!"

They smiled and nodded, so I continued.

"Have you ever heard of a guy named Nicodemus?"

They shook their heads.

"Well, he was a religious leader during the time of Jesus, but he had a lot of emptiness and questions." I turned to the story in John 3 and read it out loud, sharing how Nicodemus came to Jesus one night and learned the good news of forgiveness and eternal life from Jesus Himself. "The gospel is a message of extraordinary, unconditional love. Jesus died on the cross and gave up His life because of His love for us."

Bethany reached up and swiped a hand below her eyes. *Open up her heart, Lord God.*

"Jesus has the power to pull you out of your guilt, brokenness, and shame, wash you off, and give you new life and hope. He can do that for you," I encouraged. "He loves you that much."

I reached the end of my lesson and pulled out my laptop to play a song. Within seconds, something inside Bethany broke. She released a rasping sob and curled forward, her shoulders shaking. With my own heart breaking, I stood, circled the table, and knelt on the floor next to her, putting my arms around her while she cried.

Before I entered the room, the secretary told me Bethany had done horrible things. I didn't doubt it. But in this moment, she was just a broken girl with tears running down her face and a heart being touched by Jesus.

By the time the song ended, her tears had stopped, and a little of the brokenness seemed to have left her. I never saw her again after that afternoon. I gave the staff a Bible and a note I'd written to give her when she was released. I still pray for her, and while I didn't have the privilege of leading her to Jesus, I believe God brought us together that day for a purpose. I'm trusting He planted a few seeds. Maybe one day I'll see the big picture, but for now, I'm thankful I had the chance to tell her about Jesus. I did my part, and I trust God to complete the work He started.

Bethany isn't the only shattered girl I've knelt beside on a jail floor. What I've learned by meeting these girls is that everyone has a story, and it's usually marked with pain, brokenness, and more than a few moments of hopelessness. But you don't have to start a prison ministry to encounter these stories. They're everywhere. And only one person has the power to rewrite them into messages of hope and redemption. His name is Jesus.

God is unique in how He pursues us. He doesn't follow a formula, and He'll stop at nothing to reach the world with His love. He knows how to break through to the people around us, and He wants to use us—if we'll let Him. All we have to do is obey when He calls, love at all times, pray hard, speak truth, boldly proclaim God's good news, and leave the results to Him.

It's Worth It

I'm reminded of the story of Robert J. Thomas. In the late 1800s, God called him to be one of the first missionaries to Korea. His first trip was short and mostly spent learning about the people and their language. His second trip was supposed to be long-term, but upon arrival in the city of Pyongyang, his ship was attacked by Korean soldiers, and Robert was murdered. He never started one church or led one Korean to Christ.[4] Most would consider his ministry and endeavors a waste.

But God still used him. When the soldiers attacked, Robert had a few Korean Bibles which he begged them to take, crying out "Jesus, Jesus!" in their language. After he died, the soldiers who killed him took the Bibles. Years later, a house was discovered in the area, wallpapered with the pages of Scripture. People came from all over to read the walls, discover the God that one man was willing to die for, and learn about the gospel that prompted him to leave his home and travel thousands of miles to save the people who killed him. Today, individuals in certain parts of North Korea secretly worship God, but the gospel is still spreading—all because of one "failed" missionary and the Bible he brought.

The gospel is worth the cost of our discomfort. It's worth the cost of our fears and anxieties. It's worth giving up time, energy, and even our lives. The world is desperate for a touch from God, and in this generation of darkness, it's only going to get it if we, the light bearers, will walk among them and shine the light of the One we follow. What our world needs is revival. True revival starts on our knees, crying out for a touch from heaven that God would pour out His spirit upon this sin-soaked ground. Revival starts one life at a time. It happens when we surrender our own plans and let God invade our hearts and use our lives to spread the news that Jesus Christ is risen. That is the gospel and the heart of a true witness for Jesus. That is a message worth sharing.

In 2016, Pedro was diagnosed with stomach cancer. His family and friends prayed fervently for God's healing. Even as he battled cancer, his passion for Christ never wavered. Every day in the hospital he told his nurses that his daily goal was to tell someone about Jesus. And he did. As long as there was breath in his lungs, he told the doctors, nurses, nurse's aides, janitorial workers, kitchen staff, and anyone he could about Christ. Lying in that hospital bed, Pedro led a nurse and a nurse's aide to the Lord. His body was weakening, but his passion for Christ continued to grow.

In April of that year, God answered many prayers for healing by drawing Pedro into His presence. Finally, the faithful servant, who told everyone he could about Jesus, came face-to-face with the Savior who changed every part of his life.

I know without a doubt Pedro heard the words, "Well done, good and faithful servant" (Matt. 25:23 NIV).

That's how you share the gospel. One person—one heart, one life—at a time.

It Only Takes 120

The most beautiful part of sharing the gospel is that we get to join in Jesus's story of redemption. It takes us a step beyond accepting Christ and places us in the pages of the next chapter. Imagine this. *You* could be the person who invites someone into the presence of God. *You* could be the person who God handpicked to draw a soul to heaven. Isn't that incredible?

My prayer for our generation is that we fall deeply in love with Jesus and grow passionate about the gospel. I pray He sweeps us off our feet with the beauty of His sacrifice and sets a fire in our souls to share Him with others.

The baton is in our hands. The greatest message in the world has been passed to us. As the next generation, we're responsible for sharing it with generations to come.

Will we?

Will we have the boldness and singleness of mind and heart? Will we look to the cross and be flooded with passion for Christ? Or will we let the fire die because of our apathy, self-focus, and fear?

When Jesus ascended into heaven and commissioned all believers to go out and make disciples, the number of Christ followers was small. Acts 1:15 says that "the number of names was about a hundred and twenty."

One hundred and twenty.

That's it.

I don't know if there were more people who followed Christ and would go out and preach the gospel, but the Bible follows the story of this one hundred and twenty. And that's all that was needed to begin building the church. It makes me wonder, *If there were only one hundred and twenty Christians left in the world today, would the gospel spread and flourish as it did then? Or would it die out?*

While I know God would never let that happen, it's still a sobering question based on the state of our culture and how seriously we take our commission.

A few pages later in Acts, we see the Holy Spirit filling these disciples, and we hear of the miracles and works that followed. The world saw the difference. They wondered what it was.

Even though Jesus was no longer present in body, He was the answer. Because of the Holy Spirit's power and the disciples' testimonies, the gospel spread across the globe.

And it started with just one hundred and twenty faithful followers.

That's God. Only He could bring such explosive growth.

And He can do it again. He can use us. More importantly, He *wants* to use us.

We just have to be bold enough to open our mouths and proclaim the best news the world has ever heard and faithful enough to go out, speak out, and love with our lives. Like Billy Graham said, "God proved his love on the Cross. When Christ hung, and bled, and died, it was God saying to the world, 'I love you.'"[5]

Let's share that love. Let's live like it's true.

Lord, set our hearts on fire for the gospel!

— Going Deeper —

1. What most inspired you about Pedro's story? Why do you think he was so passionate about sharing the gospel?

2. Have you ever shared the gospel? If so, how did you do it and how did it go?

3. Have you ever said no when God asked you to share the gospel? Why? What do you think might have happened if you had?

4. Can you relate to how hard sharing the gospel is? How can you move past your fear and be faithful with this message?

5. What do you think would happen if there were only one hundred and twenty Christians left today? Stop and pray right now for God to give you the strength to be faithful with the gospel. Look for opportunities this week and follow through when God brings them.

14

no reserves, no retreats, no regrets

radical conviction 101

While doing research for this book, I came across a Wiki-How article titled, "How to Be a Great Christian Teenager: Thirteen Steps."[1]

I hadn't known WikiHow was an expert on Christianity, but the title seemed promising so I followed the link and started reading. First step: "Be Reasonable and Considerate."

Hmm, interesting step one, I thought.

The steps continued with tips like taking your Bible with you everywhere you went and attending every service your church holds. They went on like that until I reached step nine: "If you have not already, then get saved."

My jaw dropped. Step *nine*? Seriously?

While the article contained some truth and the author meant well, it painted a picture of how we've diluted following God.

Somehow we've been able to condense it into a thirteen-step process. But following God means more than being reasonable and considerate and carrying our Bibles everywhere we go. The article spoke nothing of sacrifice, surrender, or passionate love for Jesus.

We started this book by diagnosing the problem, moved on to the solution, and after that (at the risk of sounding like a WikiHow article) zoomed in and focused on individual problems and topics.

Now I want to zoom back out and take another look at the big picture. Let's refresh our perspective and get back to the heart of following Christ. Because it's so much more than a thirteen-step process.

A Millionaire Missionary

William Borden was just a sixteen-year-old going on a trip around the world. His parents were wealthy Chicago elite in the early 1900s, and a worldwide tour was their idea of a graduation present.

But God had bigger plans.

As William traveled through Europe, Asia, and the Middle East, God placed a call on his heart—to leave behind the life of privilege he'd always known and share the gospel with those who had never heard about Christ. During that trip, William wrote two words in his Bible.

No reserves.

When he came home, his parents insisted he attend college as planned. He enrolled at Yale and soon discovered that most of his fellow students didn't have the same passion or goals as he did. One of his friends even criticized him and said he was "throwing himself away as a missionary."[2]

William wasn't deterred. He began meeting with a friend every morning to pray and read the Bible, and soon those morning meetings expanded and lit a campuswide revival. By the time William was a senior, one thousand of Yale's thirteen hundred students were meeting in such groups. He wrote in his journal, "Say no to self and yes to Jesus every time."[3]

He also worked with the homeless, founded a rescue mission, and served on its staff. His passion for Christ impacted everyone he met. When one tourist to the area was asked what had impressed him most, he replied, "The sight of that young millionaire kneeling in prayer beside a bum at the Yale Hope Mission."[4]

After graduating from Yale, William wrote two more words in his Bible.

No retreats.

Now graduated, he started working toward going to China, where he felt called to serve. Before heading there, however, William first went to Egypt to learn the Arabic language and prepare for life as a missionary to Muslims. While he was there, he contracted spinal meningitis and died less than a month later at the age of twenty-five. Just before his death, he wrote two more words in his Bible.

No regrets.

Even though he was young and didn't make it to the mission field, William aspired to live sold out for Christ. As a result, his story has inspired countless people to live for Christ with no reserves. No retreats. And ultimately, no regrets.

When I first heard these three phrases, they struck my heart as the core of a true Christ follower. We don't hold back. We don't look back. We give all, we stand firm, and we press on until the very end.

No Reserves: Give All

In the book of Mark, there's a story of a man who was young, rich, and powerful. He had the world at his fingertips and everything he could want.

But he knew it wasn't enough. There was an aching in his soul that not even his riches could fill. He craved what the man named Jesus said He could offer: *eternal life.*

So the next time Jesus passed through Judea, this rich young ruler thought, *This is my chance.* He ran to Him and knelt. "Good Teacher, what shall I do that I may inherit eternal life?" (Mark 10:17).

"If you want to enter into life, keep the commandments," Jesus replied.

"Which ones?" The young man asked. He needed to know . . . was he doing enough?

Jesus listed several of the Ten Commandments. Hope flared in the man's soul. And yet, he replied, "All these things I have kept from my youth. What do I still lack?" Because he knew *something* was still missing.

Jesus answered, "One thing you lack: Go your way, sell whatever you have and give to the poor, and you will have treasure in heaven; and come, take up the cross, and follow Me" (Mark 10:21).

His soul plummeted. Sell all he had? Walk away from it? His life, his comforts, his power, his prestige, and his wealth? Deep in his heart, he sensed this was the answer. This was what he longed for during those sleepless nights and purposeless days. And yet . . . it was too much to ask. It hit him too hard.

He couldn't give that much.

So he walked away, his heart sorrowful but riches intact. His house full. His soul empty.[5]

As teenagers, we're often a lot like this young man. We have a longing for Jesus, but we want to negotiate the stakes. We want to be in control of how much following Him costs. We want all the benefits without the sacrifice.

And when Jesus asks us to go deeper, we walk away and say it's too much. Too hard. Too costly.

Like the rich young ruler, we're more than willing to *do*—what good thing shall I *do*?—but we're not as willing to *give*. Especially when it strikes at the heart of what we cherish most. Like some of us, this young man had kept all the commandments from his youth.

But Jesus still said he lacked something.

What are you holding back? What's keeping you from whole-heartedly following Christ? Do you believe Jesus is enough? Or does it have to be Jesus . . . and your family? Jesus . . . and your friends? Jesus . . . and your modern comforts? What if it was just . . . *Jesus*?

No Retreats: Stand Firm

In Luke 9, we meet a man with good intentions but weak commitment. While talking to Jesus, he said, "Lord, I will follow You, but let me first go and bid them farewell who are at my house" (v. 61).

That seemed perfectly reasonable to me at first glance. But there's more going on than we realize. Commentators suggest that a better translation would say something like, "Let me go put my house in order." If that's the case, he wasn't asking for a quick goodbye with his family but a postponement to actually following Christ. One commentator says, "There is what has the appearance of a spontaneous offer, coupled with a plea for postponement."[6] In other words, he didn't think it through and wanted a delay.

Like this man, we're quick to say, "Jesus, I'll follow You." And then we realize what that actually means, so we tack on a "but" to soften the level of commitment.

Jesus, I'll follow You . . . but first let me graduate from high school.

Jesus, I'll follow You . . . but don't ask me to save sex for marriage.

Jesus, I'll follow You . . . but first let me settle down and get married.

Jesus, I'll follow You . . . but don't ask me to serve You in another country.

Jesus, I'll follow You . . . but leave what I do with my free time alone.

Jesus is asking us not to look back. Not to retreat on our original commitment of "Jesus, I'll follow You."

No retreats means going the distance with God. When we first set out to follow Christ, we had no idea where our commitment could lead us. For many, it's led to death, persecution, torture, ridicule, and unfathomable suffering. For some, it's led to giving up all they owned and moving to another country. For all, it's led to sacrifices, great or small. He doesn't give us the map or show us what the future will hold. He gives one command: *follow Me.*

I'm inspired and humbled by the stories of brave men and women who said "Yes! I love Him more than life itself!" and were willing to lay everything on the line.

Men like eighteen-year-old Ivan Moiseyev, who refused to be re-educated and talked out of his beliefs in God by the Communists in 1970s USSR. When interrogated over his refusal to give the "correct" communist answers in order to be freed, Ivan replied, "Sometimes there is a difference between the correct answers and the true ones. Sometimes God does not permit me to give the 'correct' answers."[7] When his interrogators encountered his unswerving faith, they attempted to break him in a myriad of different ways—forcing him to stand outside all night in negative-degree weather, putting him in refrigerated cells, brainwashing him, and finally beating and stabbing him to death.

Ivan didn't have superhuman strength or resistance. In fact, he feared his own weakness. In a letter to his parents not long before he was killed, he wrote,

> The Lord has showed the way to me . . . and I have decided to follow it . . . I will now have more severe and bigger battles than I have had till now. But I do not fear them. He goes before me. Do not grieve for me, my dear parents. It is because I love Jesus more than myself. I listen to Him, though my body does fear somewhat and does not wish to go through everything. I do this because I do not value my life as much as I value Him. And I will not await my own will, but I will follow as the Lord leads. He says, Go, and I go.[8]

I also think of women like Aida Skripnikova who, in 1961, faced her first imprisonment at the age of nineteen for passing out poems she'd written about Jesus. Persecution was fierce in the Communist Soviet Union and even something as innocent as a poem was considered a threat. After being released, Aida went straight back to her work in the underground church. She wrote, "We cannot be silent about what constitutes the whole meaning of our life—about Christ."[9] Christ truly was the central focus of her life, and by the age of twenty-seven, Aida was facing her fourth prison term. She was released after three more years, but the stunning beauty of her youth was gone forever, worn away by the years of hardship and suffering. Despite the hardship Aida faced, one thing never changed—her passion for Christ and the joy and love for her Savior that was uncrushed by the suffering and pain.

And finally, I think of men and women like Vang and Mee, who are serving God right now in Southeast Asia with the full knowledge that they could be arrested or even killed for Christ any day. Both have had attempts on their lives. A few months after Mee committed her life to Christ, a man in her village pointed a gun to her head and said, "If you continue to be a Christian, I will kill you now." She boldly replied, "You can kill my body but not my spirit."[10] The man lowered his gun and left. Right now, Vang and Mee lead an illegal house church and share Christ with everyone they can. They know the risks, but in Mee's words, "It would be an honor to die for God."[11] To them, there is no such thing as a "safe faith."

These are only three stories out of millions. All around the world, Christians are suffering and dying for Jesus because they refuse to deny His name. To suffer for Him is their privilege. They will do no less than give their all. Hebrews 12:1-2 says, "Therefore we also, since we are surrounded by so great a cloud of witnesses, let us lay aside every weight, and the sin which so easily ensnares us, and let us run with endurance the race that is set before us, looking unto Jesus."

As the verse states, we're "surrounded by so great a cloud of witnesses." How can we do any less than these brave brothers and sisters in Christ who have been willing to give their all for Jesus?

We currently live in a free nation. The risk of following Christ may not be as great in America as it is in other countries, but that doesn't mean we're not called to give our all. The point isn't whether we would *die* for Him, but whether we're *living* for Him. In their book, *Jesus Freaks*, DC Talk said, "Some Christians haven't even attempted to think about whether or not they would die for Jesus because they haven't really been living for Him."[12] May we never give up our freedom to live all-out for Christ when martyrs are daily standing firm in the face of death.

I can't help but ask myself, *When have I retreated?* Because I know I have. I've let fear overtake my faith. I've said no and turned away. I've looked back. I've retreated when I compromised and said, or did, something I knew wasn't right.

But from now on I say no more. Let's be a generation that lives for Christ with no retreats and holy stubbornness.

When He asks us to share the gospel: *no retreats.*

When He asks us to stand firm and speak out, even on unpopular topics: *no retreats.*

When He asks us to sit down and take the time to love someone: *no retreats.*

And even if He asks us to lay down our lives: *no retreats.*

I want to have the kind of love for Jesus to boldly look persecution, adversity, and fear in the face and unflinchingly declare, "I am a Christian."

I will not retreat.

No Regrets: Love Much

Regret is a hard thing to swallow.

It leaves a bitter taste in your mouth and an ache in your heart. I've experienced regret in my life from things as small as eating chocolate cake for breakfast to things as big as not sharing the gospel with someone when God nudged my heart. But what I've never regretted, and never will, are the things I've done for Jesus. If you

181

could ask anyone who was martyred for Christ if it was worth it—all the pain, suffering, and fear—I have no doubt they'd say, "Yes, it was worth it." All the suffering on this momentary earth is eclipsed in a flash by the glory of heaven. When you live with the perspective of eternity, you know God has a purpose for your life—or your death.

One of my spiritual heroes understood this. After trial and loss and lessons in trust, she was able to embrace the truth that there are no ifs in God's kingdom. But let's start at the beginning of her story.

It was 1943. Europe was in the thick of World War II, including the Nazi-occupied Netherlands. There, in the middle of Haarlem, was a tiny watch shop run by an old man and his two unmarried daughters. For three years, they felt the oppression of the Nazi occupation, but while Europe was fighting a war resulting in death, these three individuals—Corrie, Betsie, and Father ten Boom— were fighting a battle for the sake of life. The life of the Jews.

A secret room had been built at the very top of the old shop, in Corrie's bedroom. Underground resistance cells were formed and a trickle of Jewish "guests" began to find refuge in the "hiding place." Hundreds of displaced Jews passed through the tiny shop, each one a precious member of God's chosen people. The ten Booms knew the risk they were taking. Every day they walked a knife's edge of discovery, but they trusted that God's angels surrounded them.

On February 28, 1944, everything unraveled. The Gestapo raided the shop, and though all the Jews made it to the secret room, Corrie, Betsie, and their father were arrested and taken to the Gestapo headquarters and then Scheveningen Prison. As they entered the headquarters, one of the chief interrogators saw Father ten Boom and called him over. "I'd like to send you home, old fellow," he said. "I'll take your word that you won't cause any more trouble."[13]

"If I go home today," he said evenly and clearly, "tomorrow I will open my door again to any man in need who knocks."[14]

He died ten days later in prison.

Corrie and Betsie spent four months in Scheveningen before being transferred to Vught and then Ravensbrück, a women's camp as infamous as it was deadly. There the sisters encountered cold and exhaustion and flea-ridden barracks. They saw death and unspeakable atrocities and starvation and pain. But through it all, they never lost faith in God. They created a pocket of light in a place of deepest darkness and saw God's hand at work even in Ravensbrück. God worked miracles by providing a bottomless bottle of vitamins and allowing them to keep their Bible hidden from the guards. Corrie and Betsie gave hope to the women around them, led many to Christ, and dreamed of the day when they could tell the world the truth they'd learned. "There is no pit so deep that He is not deeper still." [15]

On a cold December day, after several months at Ravensbrück, Betsie passed into the arms of the One she loved most, a smile on her face and peace in her heart. Heartbroken over the loss of her beloved sister, Corrie still clung to Jesus and told everyone she could about Betsie's unwavering faith. Fifteen days later, Corrie was released in yet another miracle, this time in the form of a clerical error. A week after she left Ravensbrück, all the women her age were put to death.

God had plans for Corrie. To tell the world about the hope she'd found in Jesus. That even though she'd lost everything, she had no regrets and indeed, would do it over again. "There are no 'ifs' in God's kingdom," Corrie wrote in her famous book *The Hiding Place*. "His timing is perfect. His will is our hiding place."[16]

Few stories have inspired and challenged me more than that of the Ten Booms. Their lives revolved around their one great love and nothing—not the power of the Nazis or the darkness of a concentration camp or even death itself—could change that.

They believed Jesus gave everything for them and that they were called to follow Him, no matter the consequences. As they walked naked through Ravensbrück, they joined in the fellowship of His sufferings and remembered that "they took *His* clothes too."[17] As

Betsie was beaten for not working fast enough, she remembered how Christ was beaten for them. "Look at Jesus only,"[18] she said.

They lived sold out for their Lord, and they had no regrets.

I can't help but wonder what would happen if we lived like that? If we lived dedicated to Jesus, willing to give our all for Him because we know He gave His all for us. He didn't hold back. He didn't retreat. He gave everything, because of His great love for us.

Will we give Him everything because of our great love for Him?

Love is what spurs us on to live fully for Christ. *Love* is what leads us to live with radical conviction and unwavering devotion. We love because we were first loved. Because nothing can separate us from the love of Christ. Because our salvation was bought with liquid love—the blood of our Savior.

That's what following Jesus is all about. It's not a thirteen-step process to become a "great Christian teen." It's reawakening a dying love in our hearts and learning to live for Christ . . . or die for Christ. With no reserves. No retreats . No regrets.

— Going Deeper —

1. What does living with no reserves mean for you?
2. Have you ever retreated? What happened and why? If you could do it over, what would you do differently?
3. Can you imagine a life with no regrets? How can you live for Christ so you have no regrets?
4. How far would you be willing to go for Christ? How do the examples of what others have given for Him inspire or convict you?
5. Which story in this chapter inspired you most? Why?

conclusion

definition of a rioter

I waited as each person stuck their hand in the box, pulled out a slip of paper, and answered the question before passing it on. Finished with her turn, my sister slid the box my way. I picked the first card off the stack and sucked in a breath as I read the question on the back.

We'd just finished dinner, and as usual, the couple hosting our young adult small group pulled out their dinner conversation cards. Throughout the meeting, we'd answered both strange and poignant questions, but this one tugged at my heart fiercely.

"Wow," I whispered. I looked up at everyone around the table. "Umm, how long do I have again?" I asked, half-joking. I read the question out loud, "If Jesus had one message for today's youth, what would it be?"

I tried to keep my answer as short as possible, but the question stayed in my heart long after Amanda and I bundled into our coats and drove home through the snow.

If Jesus had one message for today's youth, what would it be?

The answer has been repackaged countless times. Some might say His message would be about basing our identity in Christ. Others might say it would be about relationships or media use or even something to do with our spiritual disciplines. Each of those answers would contain truth. But I believe it comes down to the same answer Jesus gave when He was asked a similar question.

In Mark 12, the Pharisees and Sadducees threw question after question at Jesus. The scribes listened to these debates and heard the Pharisees and Sadducees reasoning among themselves as they walked away. Jesus apparently answered the questions well since the Pharisees and Sadducees hadn't been able to trap Him in His words as they'd hoped. One of the scribes came to Jesus with a question of his own: "Which is the first commandment of all?"

He answered, "The Lord our God, the Lord is one. And you shall love the LORD your God with all your heart, with all your soul, with all your mind, and with all your strength.' This is the first commandment" (Mark 12:29–30).

We've come full circle. Following Christ is a pattern that always comes back to, and is paved with, love. This love for Christ overtakes and transforms our lives. It alters the way we think, speak, act, and relate to those around us. It turns our lives into living sacrifices of worship, as we're overwhelmed with His love for us. That's why Jesus didn't tell the scribe to follow a list of rules or obey a certain commandment. Without love for God, we have nothing.

Even the scribe who asked Jesus that question understood this. He replied, "Well said, Teacher. You have spoken the truth, for there is one God, and there is no other but He. And to love Him with all the heart, with all the understanding, with all the soul, and with all the strength, and to love one's neighbor as oneself is more than all the whole burnt offerings and sacrifices" (Mark 12:32–33).

Loving God with our heart, soul, strength, and mind encompasses every aspect of our lives, from our emotions and affections

186

to our wills to every thought we think and thing we do. We love Him with our all. There is no part of our lives we hold back.

That unreserved, passionate devotion is worth more than anything else we could offer. More than legalism and rules. More than outward actions without inward change. More than our attempts at perfection. Remember, God doesn't need perfect people, but He does want passionate people.

That's what I believe Jesus's message is for today's youth: *Love Me with all your heart, all your soul, all your mind, and all your strength.*

Keep on the Journey

We've come a long way, you and I. We've learned who God is and how He changes everything. How He's worth everything. We've gone on a journey together, but now that we're nearing the finish, don't let the end of this book be the end of your voyage with God. Don't make this book the journey but rather the beginning of the journey and the challenge you need to keep going and stay strong to the end.

This love riot is only the launching pad—the explosion that ignites a relentless commitment and unswerving love for God. This is only the call of "On your mark. Get set. Go!" There's still a race ahead.

If we could meet and talk over coffee (a caramel mocha for me, please), there's one thing I would want to speak into your heart and encourage you to do: keep falling in love with Jesus and continue drawing near to Him. I hope this book has led you to love Him more, but please don't stop. Keep following hard after Him. Keep digging into Scripture, searching and studying the Word. Keep sitting at Jesus's feet, praying, praising, and seeking hard. Keep loving the least of these and being a light in the darkness as you proclaim the good news. As you do, I pray that your love for Christ grows and thrives, exploding in your heart and overtaking your life. Jesus is worth it. He is worth *everything*.

This journey won't be easy. It's a constant struggle and a continual battle. There will be days you'll feel like giving up, and moments when you'll wonder if it's all worth it. You may even wonder if God is really loving and good. You'll have times of doubt and fear. It's easy to get discouraged and weary. The enemy will attempt to tell you you're not good enough. That it's no use. That you're too far gone. He may even be whispering those lies in your heart right now, telling you you're not getting it or that this message doesn't apply to you or that this book isn't for you.

Don't listen to the lies. We're all broken. But in Christ, we're redeemed. We all fail. But through Jesus, we're forgiven.

I know it's not easy, which is why I've been praying for you. I pray God strengthens you and gives you a love for Himself like you've never experienced before. I've written a prayer for you below, much of it taken from Scripture. Pray it over yourself. But don't stop there. Pull out your Bible and pray the words of Scripture over your life. Believe them and let their truth transform you.

Dear Jesus,

Thank You for relentlessly pursuing me. Thank You that nothing can separate me from Your love. Strengthen me, Lord God, and equip me to follow hard after You. I choose You, Jesus. I'm all-in. I won't look back, second guess, or retreat. I will stand firm on the Rock and build upon Your truth.

Help me stand strong in the face of persecution. No matter what trials or difficult decisions may come, help me to always rejoice that I am counted worthy to suffer for Your name. Help me to be salt and light to a broken and dark world and walk wisely, using the time You've given me to advance Your kingdom. Help me follow You—no matter what.

I pick up the sword of the Spirit—which is Your Word. Teach me to use it. Lead me to a knowledge of the truth. Give me a passionate love for Your Word. Clothe me with the armor You've given me, and teach me to fight through Your Holy Spirit power.

When I'm tempted to give up, bring me back to the foot of the cross—where You didn't give up but went to the point of death to show me Your extravagant love. And above all, give me more of Yourself, and help me fall in love with You. Help me to pick up my cross and follow You, radically and wholeheartedly. Help me love You with all my heart, soul, strength, and mind. Jesus, You are my everything. I love You. Amen.[1]

There's a New Generation Arising

Hebrews 12:1–2 compares following Jesus to running a race. It encourages us to "run with endurance the race that is set before us, looking unto Jesus, the author and finisher of our faith, who for the joy that was set before Him endured the cross, despising the shame, and has sat down at the right hand of the throne of God."

I pray we learn to "run with endurance" looking only to Jesus. I pray that we rely on only Him and His shed blood to give us strength and bring us across the finish line. And at the end of our lives, I pray that we will be able to say with Paul, "I have fought the good fight, I have finished the race, I have kept the faith" (2 Tim. 4:7).

God has not given up on our generation. On the contrary, I believe He has more in store for us than we can imagine. I believe the power which rose Jesus Christ from the dead can raise up the spiritually dying remains of this generation and spark a passion in our souls for His name. In a culture announcing that teenagers are leaving the church, I know God can flip the paradigm and bring us back. Can you imagine a society filled with teens on fire for Jesus Christ? Can you imagine churches packed with teens devoted to God? Can you imagine communities overflowing with teens committed to following Christ and working to bring His kingdom to glory in the years to come?

I can.

That is my vision, and I'm daring enough to believe God can do it. He can and will and has done it in the past—and He can do it again.

So come, join the love riot. Let's live all-in for Christ. With radical devotion and passionate adoration of our Savior. Let's go out and show the world the God we know. Let's share the gospel and serve our neighbors and live in wonderstruck worship of our King. Let's live like Jesus Christ is Lord. Like He's everything.

Because He is, you know.

There's a new generation arising.

Some call us crazy and radical. Others might refer to us as Jesus freaks. We're the heartbeat of this century. The world sometimes thinks we're missing out, but we know that's not true. We have our sights set on the goal, and we're running the race with our eyes fixed on Jesus. We won't give up. We won't turn back. We're devoted, wholly committed, and in love with the Savior of our souls.

Who are we?

We're passionate followers of Jesus Christ.

— Going Deeper —

1. What do *you* think is the one message Jesus has for today's youth?
2. Why do you think Jesus told the scribe that to love God with all your heart, soul, mind, and strength is the first and greatest commandment? How does love for God transform every other area of your life?
3. Why do you think following Jesus is like running a race? What are some practical steps you can take to keep you on course (e.g., daily Scripture reading, prayer, etc.)?

4. How has this book altered your perspective about God and wholeheartedly living for Him? What stood out to you?

5. What did you learn from this book and what practical application can you start applying today to keep moving forward on the journey of wholeheartedly following Christ?

acknowledgments

Several months into writing the first draft of this book, I was talking with a friend on the phone. It had been a rough few months of pounding out words through fear and anxiety, feeling inadequate, and wondering why God would want *me* to write a book. After listening to my struggles and encouraging me, my friend asked if she could pray over me that very moment. Of course I said yes, so she began reaching out to God on my behalf. As she prayed, one of the words she used jumped out and struck my heart: *collaboration*. I was trying to write this book on my own. Her prayer helped me realize I didn't have to. Not only did I have an army of prayer warriors and supporters behind me but I was also in a collaboration with the greatest Author of all time—God Himself.

While the journey wasn't easy, He brought me across the finish line with the helping hands of so many along the way. I have seen His grace and His hand at work, and I'm thankful for all the amazing people He's brought into my life. I couldn't have done it without them.

Mom, I have no words to describe how much you mean to me! I've learned more from you than any other person on earth, and

I'm blessed by you in so many ways. You give of yourself daily to help others, and I'm so thankful for all the ways you help me. From editing my very first articles (and not being afraid to mark them up with a red pen!) to taking me to conferences, teaching me about Jesus, and praying for me so faithfully, you've impacted me and this book in innumerable ways. I'm beyond blessed and honored to call you my mama! I love you so much!

Amanda, you're the best sister ever. Seriously. I love you so very much and I'm constantly blessed by you. Thank you for encouraging me along the way and always being there for me—even when I'm a mess. Thank you for reading every chapter multiple times, brainstorming ideas, and praying for me. You're the Tolkien to my Lewis—we're the Inklings, version 2.0—and my best friend. I'm so thankful for you, and I praise God for the blessing you are!

Dad, thanks for always asking about my writing when I'm sure you'd rather talk about tools or airplanes. Thank you for all you do. I couldn't do this without you! I love you!

Grandma, thank you for your amazing support of my writing and all your encouragement. It blesses me so much!

A huge thanks to Brett and Ana Harris. Brett, you've impacted me and my writing more than you know! When I first read *Do Hard Things*, I knew it would be influential in my life, but I never dreamed one of the authors—you!—would play such a huge role in guiding my own writing. Thank you for being such a wonderful coach and "big brother" and for writing the foreword for this book. I'm truly honored.

Ana, thank you for taking the time to read the manuscript and offer so much thoughtful feedback. This book is truly stronger and more grace-filled because of it and I appreciate your insight greatly! I've learned so much from both of you about writing but also about faith, perseverance, integrity, and of course, doing hard things.

Jaquelle Crowe Ferris, you were the first professional to encourage me in my writing. Thank you for publishing me on *The*

Rebelution, for putting up with my endless submissions, and for cheering me on! You'll never know how much your encouragement helped me to keep going.

Is it strange to thank a website? Well, I'm going to anyway. Thank you to *The Rebelution* and the beautiful community of "rebelutionaries" there. Thanks also to the amazing team I get to work with—Christopher, Katherine, Isabelle, Bella, and all our writers and readers. You're the best!

Dan Balow and Steve Laube, not many writers get to work with two such incredible agents . . . but I did! Dan, thank you for taking a chance on a clueless young girl at a writers' conference and for sticking with me through all the rejections. Steve, thank you for all your encouragement and advice. I'm so thrilled we get to work together!

Rebekah Guzman, thank you for seeing the potential in my book. You're an answer to prayer and I'm still shocked—and excited and blessed!—that I get to work with you! It's an honor and a privilege.

Thank you, Nicci Jordan Hubert, for doing such an incredible job with developmental editing. I was nervous about the editing process, but you made it fun and easy! You made the book tighter and stronger. . . I couldn't ask for a better editor!

Many thanks to Robin Turici for your amazing, spot-on edits. Thank you for not freaking out when I told you I wanted to cut an entire chapter and restructure large portions of the book so far into the editing process. Working with you was a joy!

To the entire Baker Books team, I don't know all your names, but I do know you rock. Thank you for helping bring this book to life. I'm over-the-moon excited to work with each and every one of you!

A huge thank you to my sweet friend Tabitha. Your many prayers have sustained and encouraged me more than you know! Thank you for all the four-hour phone calls, hundreds of messages, and dozens of letters. You're such an encourager and prayer

warrior, and I cannot wait to see what God has in store for you
. . . it's going to be amazing. Hugs, friend!

I'm grateful to Anna and Dan for reading the first few chapters
and sharing your thoughts. Your insights made the book stronger.
Anna, thank you for all your prayers and allowing me to share
your testimony!

Much thanks to Preston and Olivia. Preston, you read the
longest, most unedited version and still managed to say it reminded you of *Crazy Love*. Your kind encouragement made my
~~day week~~ month. Olivia, thank you for your many prayers and
sweet friendship.

To the amazing prayer warriors behind me—"Grandma" Wes-
theim, I truly feel your prayers helped "birth" this book. Betty,
thank you for all your encouragement and countless prayers.
You're both an inspiration to me!

Thank you, Schuyler and Carrie-Grace, for your prayers and
sweet friendship! Carrie-Grace, you got one of the first sneak
previews. Shhh, don't tell.

"Aunt" Jocelyn, thank you for your encouraging texts and
prayers. I can't tell you how much they mean to me! Thank you
also for allowing me to share your dad's story. I consider it a
tremendous honor and one I don't take lightly.

Special gratitude to the Thomas family for giving me permission
to share Jeremiah's story. I pray God uses it and I'm humbled to
have the opportunity to share his bravery and passion with others.

Finally, big thanks to YOU—the person on the other side of
the page. If you actually made it this far in the acknowledgments,
you're my friend for life. (Extra points if you read the acknowledgments *before* you read the book—I always do! It's a writer thing.)
I'm beyond humbled to imagine you reading these words. It's
crazy and surreal, and I can't thank God enough for the chance
to share what He's taught me (and is still teaching me). I pray
He uses this book to draw you nearer to Him. Please, don't ever
stop seeking Jesus!

And lastly, but mostly, thank You, Jesus. You are my hope, my love, my Lord, my Savior, my everything. I'm in awe of Your love. Thank You for dying to set me free, for calling me Your daughter, for strengthening me every day, for loving me so well. I'm a mess but You've placed a message in my heart. I'm broken but You've healed all that's shattered. Through my fear, anxiety, confusion, and heartache, You are faithful to bring me peace, confidence, clarity, and joy. All praise and honor to You! Be glorified, Lord. This is Your book. Thank You for letting me write it.

notes

Foreword

1. Alex and Brett Harris, "A Challenge for My Generation," *The Rebelution* (blog), August 8, 2005, https://www.therebelution.com/blog/2005/08/the-rebelution-a-challenge-for-my-generation/.

2. "How Old was David When _____?" Got Questions, accessed October 8, 2019, https://www.gotquestions.org/how-old-was-David.html.

3. "Who was Jeremiah in the Bible?" Got Questions, accessed October 8, 2019, https://www.gotquestions.org/life-Jeremiah.html.

4. "How Old were Jesus' Disciples?" Got Questions, accessed October 8, 2019, https://www.gotquestions.org/how-old-were-Jesus-disciples.html.

Introduction

1. Elisabeth Elliot, *Through Gates of Splendor* (New York: Harper & Brothers, 1957), 50–51.

Chapter 1 Revealing the Counterfeit

1. Barna Group, "Six Reasons Young Christians Leave Church," Barna, September 27, 2011, https://www.barna.com/research/six-reasons-young-christians-leave-church/.

2. Francis Chan, *Crazy Love* (Colorado Springs: David C Cook, 2008), 172.

3. C. S. Lewis, *Mere Christianity*, rev. ed. (New York: HarperOne, 2015), 51.

Chapter 2 It's Not Just a Pizza Party

1. C. S. Lewis, *Mere Christianity*, 169.

2. To read more about who God is, why He's worthy of our all, and how to build your faith, check out *The Reason for God* by Timothy Keller, *Crazy Love* by Francis Chan, and *Mere Christianity* by C. S. Lewis.

Chapter 3 I Don't Want a Facebook Jesus

1. Strong's Concordance 1097, Biblehub.com, accessed April 4, 2019, https://biblehub.com/greek/1097.htm.
2. Dean Inserra, "To Reach Unsaved Christians, First Help Them Get Lost," *Christianity Today*, March 5, 2019, https://www.christianitytoday.com/pastors/2019/february-web-exclusives/to-reach-unsaved-christians-first-help-them-get-lost.html.
3. David Platt, *Follow Me* (Wheaton, Il: Tyndale, 2013), 54.
4. A. W. Tozer, *The Pursuit of God* (Camp Hill, PA: WingSpread, 2007), 26, 27.

Chapter 4 Get Ready for a Renovation

1. C. S. Lewis, *Mere Christianity*, 205.
2. Billy Graham, "Billy Graham Daily Devotion: A Daily Process," *Billy Graham Evangelical Association*, October 2, 2018, https://billygraham.org/devotion/a-daily-process/.
3. George Müller, *Autobiography of George Müller* (New Kensington, PA: Whitaker, 1996), 14, 15.
4. Müller, *Autobiography of George Müller*, 16.
5. As quoted in Roger Steer, *George Müller: Delighted in God* (Fearn, Tain, Ross-shire, Scotland: Christian Focus, 2015), 177.

Chapter 5 Free Wi-Fi Not Included

1. DC Talk, *Jesus Freaks: Revolutionaries: Stories of Revolutionaries Who Changed Their World: Fearing God, Not Man* (Bloomington: Bethany House, 2002), 4, 5.
2. Stacey Philpot, "The Boy Who Stood at the Flagpole Alone," *Her View from Home* (blog), accessed October 21, 2019, https://herviewfromhome.com/the-boy-who-stood-at-the-flag-pole-alone/.

Chapter 6 Everything Means *Everything*

1. Jim Elliot, quoted in Elisabeth Elliot, *Shadow of the Almighty: The Life and Testament of Jim Elliot* (New York: HarperCollins, 1979), 247.
2. Elliot, *Shadow of the Almighty*, 249.
3. Elliot, 241.
4. Elliot, 245.
5. Elliot, 245.
6. Elliot, 9–10.
7. Elliot, 247.
8. Luke LeFevre, "What Are You Willing to Give Up?" *All or Nothing* (blog), April 4, 2016, http://allornothingblog.com/blog/2016/4/2/what-are-you-willing-to-give-up?rq=i%20want%20more%20of%20you.

Chapter 7 Raising the Battle Cry

1. C. S. Lewis, *The Screwtape Letters* (New York: HarperCollins, 1996), 2–4.

2. "Samuel Chadwick," Goodreads, accessed December 11, 2018, https://www
.goodreads.com/quotes/323811-satan-dreads-nothing-but-prayer-his-one-con
cern-is-to.

Chapter 8 Seeking Hard . . . or Hardly Seeking?

1. This idea is often attributed to Martin Luther, though its exact origins
are unknown.

Chapter 9 Deeper Than a One-Minute Devo

1. Francis Chan, *Crazy Love*, 145.

2. J. C. Ryle, *Thoughts for Young Men: Updated Edition with Study Guide* (Cedar
Lake: Waymark Books, 2018), 50.

3. For more information on persecution and where the Bible is illegal, check
out https://www.christiantoday.com/article/6-countries-where-owning-a-bible
-is-dangerous/84497.htm, https://www.persecution.com/bibles/, and https://
www.christianitytoday.com/news/2018/january/top-50-christian-persecution
-open-doors-world-watch-list.html.

Chapter 10 One Time Around Is All We've Got

1. Jeremiah Thomas, "Jeremiah's Letter to His Generation," *Operation Save
America*, June 24, 2018, http://www.operationsaveamerica.org/2018/06/24/jere
miahs-letter-to-his-generation/.

2. Thomas, "Jeremiah's Letter."

3. Thomas, "Jeremiah's Letter."

4. Thomas, "Jeremiah's Letter."

5. Jeremiah Thomas as quoted in Katelyn Brown, "Jeremiah Thomas, Age 16:
His Dying Wish to End Abortion," *The Rebelution* (blog), July 4, 2018, https://
www.therebelution.com/blog/2018/07/jeremiah-thomas-age-16-his-dying-wish
-to-end-abortion/.

6. J. C. Ryle, *Thoughts for Young Men*, 10.

7. John Koblin, "How Much Do We Love TV? Let Us Count the Ways," *New
York Times*, July 3, 2016, https://www.nytimes.com/2016/07/01/business/media
/nielsen-survey-media-viewing.html.

8. Elisabeth Elliot, *Shadow of the Almighty*, 52.

9. Jaquelle Crowe Ferris, *This Changes Everything: How the Gospel Transforms
the Teen Years* (Wheaton: Crossway, 2017), 121.

10. To learn more about Jeremiah's story, visit https://www.jeremiahstrong
.com/.

Chapter 11 Relationship Remodel

1. Burger King, Coca-Cola, Sprite, and L'Oreal in case you were wondering.

2. Timothy Keller, *The Reason for God* (New York: Penguin, 2009), 221.

Chapter 12 Social Media, TV, Technology, Oh My!

1. John Stonestreet and Brett Kunkle, *A Practical Guide to Culture* (Colorado Springs: David C Cook, 2017), 261, 262.

2. Elizabeth Chuck, "Is Social Media Contributing to Rising Teen Suicide Rate?" *NBC News*, October 22, 2017, https://www.nbcnews.com/news/us-news/social-media-contributing-rising-teen-suicide-rate-n812426.

3. Jean M. Twenge, "Have Smartphones Destroyed a Generation?" *Atlantic*, September 2017, https://www.theatlantic.com/magazine/archive/2017/09/has-the-smartphone-destroyed-a-generation/534198/.

4. Beata Mostafavi, "Does Netflix's '13 Reasons Why' Influence Teen Suicide? Survey Asks At-Risk Youths," M Health Lab, November 20, 2018, https://labblog.uofmhealth.org/rounds/does-netflixs-13-reasons-why-influence-teen-suicide-survey-asks-at-risk-youths.

5. "Sex Trafficking," *Polaris*, accessed April 12, 2019, https://polarisproject.org/human-trafficking/sex-trafficking; Tim Swarens, "How Many People are Victims of Sex Trafficking?" *Indy Star*, January 11, 2018, https://www.indystar.com/story/opinion/2018/01/11/human-trafficking-statistics-how-many-people-victims/1013877001/.

6. Christopher Witmer, "Counterintuitive Advice for Guys about Lust," *The Rebelution* (blog), January, 26, 2018, https://www.therebelution.com/blog/2018/01/counterintuitive-advice-for-guys-about-lust/.

Chapter 13 Go Out and Speak Out

1. This quote is widely attributed to St. Francis of Assisi, but it has never been confirmed. There are numerous variations from different sources, but it's unclear who actually said it first.

2. As quoted in Bobby Conway, *The Fifth Gospel: Matthew, Mark, Luke, John . . . You* (Eugene, OR: Harvest House, 2014), 9.

3. Jaquelle Crowe Ferris, "Gen Z, Let's Prioritize the Gospel as We Pursue Justice," The Gospel Coalition, May 7, 2018, https://www.thegospelcoalition.org/article/generation-z-social-justice-prioritize-gospel/.

4. DC Talk and The Voice of the Martyrs, *Jesus Freaks: Stories of Those Who Stood for Jesus: The Ultimate Jesus Freaks* (Tulsa: Albury Publishing, 1999), 295, 296.

5. Billy Graham as compiled by Debbie McDaniel, "40 Courageous Quotes from Evangelist Billy Graham," Crosswalk, accessed September 27, 2019, https://www.crosswalk.com/faith/spiritual-life/inspiring-quotes/40-courageous-quotes-from-evangelist-billy-graham.html.

Chapter 14 No Reserves, No Retreats, No Regrets

1. "How to Be a Great Christian Teenager," WikiHow, last modified July 31, 2019, https://www.wikihow.com/Be-a-Great-Christian-Teenager.

2. As quoted in "William Borden: A Life Without Regret," *Outreach Magazine*, July 8, 2018, https://outreachmagazine.com/features/discipleship/31313-william-borden-life-without-regret.html.

3. As quoted in Kyle Idleman, *Not a Fan* (Grand Rapids: Zondervan, 2011), 208.

4. As quoted in Jayson Casper, "The Forgotten Final Resting Place of William Borden," *Christianity Today*, February 24, 2017, https://www.christianitytoday.com /history/2017/february/forgotten-final-resting-place-of-william-borden.html.

5. Read the full story in Matthew 19:16–22, Mark 10:17–22, and Luke 18:18–23.

6. Ellicott's Commentary for English Readers, Biblehub.com, accessed December 17, 2018, https://biblehub.com/commentaries/ellicott/luke/9.htm.

7. As quoted in DC Talk and The Voice of the Martyrs, *Jesus Freaks* (1999), 31.

8. DC Talk, *Jesus Freaks* (1999), 35.

9. DC Talk, *Jesus Freaks* (1999), 85.

10. "Laos: Mee," Kids of Courage: *The Voice of the Martyrs*, November 6, 2018, issue 5.

11. *Voice of the Martyrs*, 6.

12. DC Talk, *Jesus Freaks* (1999), 108.

13. Corrie ten Boom, *The Hiding Place*, 35th anniversary ed. (Bloomington, MN: Chosen Books, 2006), 152.

14. Ten Boom, *The Hiding Place*, 152.

15. Ten Boom, 227.

16. Ten Boom, 234.

17. Ten Boom, 207.

18. Ten Boom, 216.

Conclusion

1. References correlate with Romans 8:38–39, Matthew 7:24, Acts 5:41, Matthew 5:13, 1 Timothy 2:4, Ephesians 6:10–18, Mark 8:34, and Matthew 22:37.

Sara Barratt is an author, speaker, avid reader, chocolate lover, and lead editor for TheRebelution.com. Her passion is challenging and encouraging teens to live sold out and set apart for Jesus. When she's not writing or dreaming up a new book idea, she loves spending time with family and friends, taking long walks, drinking copious amounts of tea, and scribbling down random thoughts that eventually get lost in her purse. Come hang out with her on Facebook, Instagram, and at her website, SaraBarratt.com.

Connect with
SARA

SARABARRATT.COM

  @SaraBarrattAuthor

theReb

rebelling against low expectations

Imagine if teens woke up in the morning energized and ready to get out of bed because they knew they had a **purpose** and were **needed** in the world.

Here's the deal, though:
It's not just a fantasy we're imagining, it's already happening.

WELCOME TO THE REBELUTION.
TheRebelution.com

LIKE THIS
BOOK?
Consider sharing it with others!

- Share or mention the book on your social media platforms. Use the hashtag **#LoveRiotBook**

- Write a book review on your blog or on a retailer site.

- Pick up a copy for friends, family, or anyone who you think would enjoy and be challenged by its message!

- Share this message on Twitter, Facebook, or Instagram: **I loved #LoveRiotBook by @SaraBarrattAuthor // @ReadBakerBooks**

- Recommend this book for your church, workplace, book club, or class.

- Follow Baker Books on social media and tell us what you like.

 **ReadBakerBooks**

 **ReadBakerBooks**

ReadBakerBooks